D1116571

THEY CALL HIM CALE

The Life and Career of NASCAR Legend Cale Yarborough

Joe McGinnis

TRIUMPH
BOOKS

Library of Congress Cataloging-in-Publication Data

McGinnis, Joe, 1954-
  They call him Cale : the life and career of NASCAR legend Cale Yarborough / Joe McGinnis.
    p. cm.
  Includes bibliographical references.
  ISBN-13: 978-1-60078-051-6
  ISBN-10: 1-60078-051-2
  1. Yarborough, Cale. 2. Automobile racing drivers—United States—Biography. 3. Stock car racing—United States—History. 4. NASCAR (Association)—History. I. Title.
  GV1032.Y36M34 2007
  796.72092—dc22
  [B]
                                                    2007041065

This book is available in quantity at special discounts for your group or organization. For further information, contact:

Triumph Books
542 South Dearborn Street
Suite 750
Chicago, Illinois 60605
(312) 939-3330
Fax (312) 663-3557

Printed in U.S.A
ISBN: 978-1-60078-051-6
Design by Chris Mulligan
Photos courtesy of AP/Wide World Photos unless otherwise indicated.

To God be the glory, great things he has done.

–Frances Jane Crosby, "To God Be the Glory"

CONTENTS

FOREWORD   vii

ACKNOWLEDGMENTS   ix

CHAPTER 1:   1
The Boy

CHAPTER 2:   23
Becoming a Man

CHAPTER 3:   57
Becoming a Racer

CHAPTER 4:   87
The Racer

CHAPTER 5:   133
The Champion

CHAPTER 6:   183
The Car Owner

CHAPTER 7:   193
The Legend

APPENDIX   205

NOTES   261

FOREWORD

Joe McGinnis takes us on a fascinating voyage into not only the life of one of America's greatest race car drivers, but also through the early days of stock-car racing and its formation.

It is also an interesting look into the South of the 1950s and how it not only formed the cultural base of a young South Carolina boy, but of NASCAR itself.

The story of Cale Yarborough furnishes the fuel of not only a legendary racer, but a unique man who overcame formidable obstacles with the help of many people, particularly his wife Betty Jo.

His story includes the time when NASCAR racers were the toughest lot in sport—bare-knuckled guys whose biggest confrontations sometimes came after the race in the tough pits of places like Sumter, Columbia, Asheville-Weaverville, Darlington, Charlotte, and Riverside. This was before multimillion-dollar salaries, jets, and rock-star buses. These guys wore blue jeans, flew beat-up prop planes, slept in fleabag motels, and drove race cars until the tires popped.

It also covers the deadly period of 1964–69, when speed outran safety and many drivers were lost in terrible crashes. To say Cale Yarborough needed courage to strap himself into one of those cars during that time is a grand understatement.

So get ready for a real literary ride through a time when legends like Richard Petty, A.J. Foyt, Mario Andretti, David Pearson, Bobby and Donnie Allison, and Darrel Waltrip found that one young driver from rural South Carolina could challenge them with a ferocity seldom seen on NASCAR's most famous tracks.

—Humpy Wheeler

ACKNOWLEDGMENTS

I would like to let my wife, Mary, my daughter, Carly, and my sons, Joseph and David, know how much I have appreciated their loving support of this effort.

I would like to especially thank Mr. Cale Yarborough and his lovely wife Betty Jo, without whose guidance and friendly cooperation this work would not have been possible.

Also, it never ceased to amaze me that everyone I talked to during the course of this work freely shared their thoughts and memories with me, whether solicited or not. All of these stories substantiated the fact that Cale has meant something special to most NASCAR fans and people throughout the racing business.

CHAPTER 1

The Boy

It's September 3, 1951. Labor Day in the Pee Dee region of South Carolina presents a brief respite from the hard summer's work. However, the town of Darlington has become a hubbub of activity. Thousands of people have laid this day of rest aside to witness the spectacle known as the Southern 500, a stock car race that, from its debut just one year prior, had already become the Indianapolis 500 of the South. Excitement filled the air, with sounds, sights, and smells that can only occur when crowds assemble to celebrate sheer competition. As the stands began to fill, a few boys from nearby Timmonsville High School searched for a parking space, anxious to join the throng. They spotted a place in a nearby field, and scattering toward the gate they called out behind them, "Remember where we parked, Cale, and we'll meet you right here after the race. And we ain't waiting on you, so you'd better be here."

Though William Caleb "Cale" Yarborough felt as if he were in a dream, he was actually at the Darlington

Raceway. It seemed as if it were the largest thing in the world. From the parking lot, the speedway looked as if it went on forever. As Cale approached the ticket booth, he began to regain control of his thoughts. He had brought enough money for the $2 ticket, but he sure didn't want to have to pay it if he didn't have to—that way he could have more money for hot dogs and Cokes. He had to figure a way inside. As he made his way past the incoming crowd, he came upon a boy handing out pamphlets, and he took one. It read:

> Darlington International Raceway today is the scene of the nation's greatest stock-car race of the year...the second annual "Southern 500" strictly stock car speed classic...under NASCAR sanction.

> Darlington, the nation's finest raceway, that's how the new mile-and-a-quarter asphalt track is regarded by the race fans throughout the country.

> Not another track in the United States of this size provides such ample facilities...a grandstand from which you can see every corner of the track from every seat... something that is better than any other track in the country.

For speed...Darlington ranks second only to Indianapolis...with its two-and-a-half mile span.

"For beauty...there's none finer than Darlington Raceway!"

Three programs were scheduled the first year...1950...with Johnny Mantz of Long Beach, California, winning the Labor Day race...then Johnny Parsons, Van Nuys, California, won the 200-mile AAA big car race...the motorcycle program that included three events was cancelled due to rain after only the novice 50-mile race saw a new record established for all tracks.

The 1951 program includes only two events—the 250-mile AAA big car race on July 4...won by Little Walt Faulkner of Long Beach, California...

So far in the three major races at Darlington Raceway, the California drivers have monopolized honors...but can they do it today?...That's the big question...and the rebels with their confederate flags flying...are out to upset the California fruit cart.

Who's your favorite today? Pick your own. Everybody else has…and they can't all be right.

Cale could wait no longer. He walked around the track until he found a place where no one was looking. He found a loose place in the fence, got down on his belly, and slid beneath. He was inside the Darlington Raceway, still had the $2 in his pocket, and was surely the happiest kid in the world.

He was inside the Darlington Raceway, still had the $2 in his pocket, and was surely the happiest kid in the world.

Cale was no stranger to auto racing. Almost every South Carolina town had a dirt track with weekly action, and Cale had been to Florence many Friday nights, clutching the fence with his dad at his side and yelling for the local heroes as they battled. Drivers whose names race fans still remember, names like Junior Johnson, Cotton Owens, and Fonty Flock. Over the course of the evening, the dirt and dust at the fence would coat you from head to toe. And, standing there at the fence, you could fix your eyes on a certain car and follow it around the track, lap after lap. You were so close that when you waved at the driver, you felt he was looking directly at you. Heck, it was almost like being in the race car.

And now here he was at Darlington! It was the biggest place Cale had ever seen. Grandstands stretched as far as he could see, and they were already almost filled. He strolled around to Turn 1 and looked across the track to Turn 4, feeling as if the other end of the track was in another country, it was so far away. And he imagined how it must feel to race around such a racetrack. Then his attention was drawn to the infield. He had never witnessed such a scene. People were everywhere. They were barbecuing, tossing footballs, eating, drinking, sleeping, laughing, and generally having the time of their lives, it seemed. From the look of it, there couldn't have been any

If there had been any question as to what he wanted to be when he grew up, he had found the answer.

beer or fried chicken left in the state of South Carolina. But then his eyes found the pits, where the race teams were preparing for the day's activities. Like a magnet, Cale immediately joined the stream of people walking across the track.

Walking straight to the pit area, he began to pick out some of the drivers whom he recognized from being at the short tracks and others whose pictures had been in the newspapers. He could see Lee Petty, Fireball Roberts, Fonty Flock, Herb Thomas, and Curtis Turner. All of his heroes together in one place, and he could walk right up to them. "Hiya, Fireball," "Hello, Fonty," he said as he would pass them. And each, in turn, waved back and answered, "Hi, kid." Cale was hooked. If there had been any question as to what he wanted to be when he grew up, he had found the answer.

Wandering from pit to pit, he was able to see and touch the race cars. Lee Petty's Plymouth, Marshall Teague's Hudson Hornet, Frank Mundy's Studebaker, and Buddy Shuman's Ford were there for his inspection. It was like being in heaven—leaning against the cars, listening to the conversation between the different teams' members as they were finishing their preparations, gazing into the engine compartments, and soaking it up like a sponge. It was very doubtful things could be any better than this.

Shortly, the time came for the race to begin, and the guards began to move the people who had made their ways from the grandstands back to their seats. Cale had to join them as they paraded back across the track, and he found a place to stand near the fence at the first turn. "Hey, kid, you can't stand there, you're blocking people's view," someone yelled to Cale. "You'll have to get in your seat or move over there out of the way." He pointed over toward the second turn, where there were nothing but bushes. Having snuck in, he had no seat, so he headed toward the bushes. Several hundred people had joined in the second turn, but there was room for one more boy. Finding a spot where the whole track was visible, he settled in. To Cale, this was as good as a box seat at the start-finish line. And the race was about to begin.

Having no particular driver as a favorite, Cale decided to root for those who were nicest to him in the pits. He waved each on, confident that they were aware of him there. There was a flat spot in the first turn, making for a lot of action in Turn 2, with cars blowing tires, spinning out, and crashing right in front of him. The cars were averaging over 100 mph, and the summer heat of 95 degrees really took its toll on tires. Most of the drivers Cale was rooting for finished the race prematurely in some spectacular way, but the racing was fierce and exciting until the end.

There was a flat spot in the first turn, making for a lot of action in Turn 2, with cars blowing tires, spinning out, and crashing right in front of him.

Herb Thomas's Hudson finished as the winner, followed by Jesse James Taylor in another Hudson and Buddy Shuman in his Ford. The race had lasted more than six-and-a-half hours because of all the caution flags, but to Cale it seemed like no time at all. He stood at the fence until all the PA announcements had been made. He listened as the announcer detailed the race's outcome, who finished in what place, and how much money they had won. He learned that 40,000 people had enjoyed the race with him. And he felt within himself that he had entered a world where he belonged. He began to dream of what he would do if he had a bunch of money. He would buy himself a Hudson for each day of the week except Sunday. Sundays being special to him, maybe he should reserve that day for a Cadillac like Red Byron's.

As the announcements ended, reality came back into focus. The other guys had said they would leave Cale if he was not back to the car on time. He'd better hurry. Realizing that he still had two dollars in his pocket, he bought a Coke and two hot dogs and headed for the parking lot. He was the first to return, so he waited…and waited…and waited for almost an hour. Shoot, he had had time to return to the pits but had missed the opportunity.

❧

The Yarborough family had deep roots in the Pee Dee region of South Carolina. Cale's Grandpa Yarborough had been quite a successful farmer, and his work ethic and business sense passed to Cale's father, Julian. Julian and his wife, Annie Mae, lived in a small wooden house just outside of Sardis, South Carolina, a small farming community of about 100 residents. Julian farmed tobacco and was also the proprietor of both the Yarborough General Store and the local cotton gin.

Cale was born on March 27, 1939, the eldest of three sons. Jerry was born two years later, and the youngest brother, J.C., followed seven years later. Their old wooden farmhouse was typical for the area, built up off the ground on pillars, with a broad front porch, screen doors held shut with springs, and a path around the back that led to the outhouse. The expansive fields around the house were as flat as panes of glass, their sandy soils filled with the nourishment needed to grow some of the best tobacco in the world. The Lynches River flowed nearby, and swampy marshes were situated around and between the fertile lands. The climate was rather temperate, with four distinct seasons, but the summer heat could reach tropical proportions.

The nurturing and encouragement Cale received there served to make him believe that there was nothing he could not do, if he wanted to.

Life was good for the Yarboroughs, but between the farm, the store, and the cotton gin, there was always work to be done. Cale was introduced at the early age of five to the rigors of the tobacco fields. He would work up and down the rows, search for tobacco worms on the broad green leaves, knock them to the ground, and stomp them. He was a friendly child, outgoing, and a favorite of the share-croppers and neighbors who were always there to help. The cotton gin became one of Cale's favorite places. Son Ham James, one of his dad's sharecroppers, worked there. Son Ham had two sons, Donnie and Willie. The three boys would play together, and when the harvest season brought the farmers to town with their crops, they would chip in and help wherever they could. The seeds would be removed from the cotton, the fibers would be bound into bales, and the seeds would be compressed for their oil. Even though Cale was always small for his age, Son Ham had soon taught him to move the big bales around the building.

Always proud of himself, Cale rushed to the store to share his new accomplishments. It was an old country store, with metal signs on the side, advertising soft drinks, chewing tobacco, and the latest remedy. The front screen door was stenciled to read "Merita Bread" in yellow and red, but there were some places where the paint was missing from people pushing the door open. There was an old stove in the middle of the store, with several wooden chairs strewn around it for the locals to gather and discuss the latest news. There was a cardboard box for the farmers to spit their tobacco juice into, but, inevitably, someone would spit on the stove. The odor of the burnt tobacco juice would rise up, giving the place a character only found in an old country store. The nurturing and encouragement Cale received there served to make him believe that there was nothing he could not do, if he wanted to.

From his first day at Sardis Grade School, Cale's favorite part of each day would be the three-mile walk. He would shuffle his feet in the dust and dream of first one adventure and then another. He was sure that he was not going to work in the dirt, but he soon found his education to be a bit boring. He was lucky enough to have the ability to pass his tests without studying much; the classroom was just a waste of time, he thought. But he learned the lesson of courage in the fourth grade, a lesson he has never forgotten. There was a big kid named Jimmy

Cale became the hero of the school, and he liked the attention.

Humphries who bullied everybody around. He was twice their size, and they were all afraid of him, especially Cale. Cale was still quite small, and was very easily intimidated. It was the first day of school, and Cale arrived at school just as the bus arrived. Cale was rushing up the school steps when he ran right into Jimmy Humphries, hard enough to knock him down. Jimmy got up, brushed himself off, and punched Cale in the face. Then he promised, "I'll give you a whipping every day." The walk to school no longer was an adventure, but more like a convicted man's last walk down the corridors of prison to his demise. Cale learned to use every trick in the book to be later than the bus in the mornings, but never said anything about it. If he arrived before the bus, he would hide

behind an oak tree until Jimmy went inside, then follow a few minutes later.

One day, as he hid behind the oak, he saw Jimmy
step from the bus, and, to his surprise, there was a
cast on Jimmy's right arm. Now was his chance. He
ran over to Jimmy, grabbed him by the left shoulder,
spun him around, and caught him with an uppercut
that sent Jimmy to the ground. Jimmy could do nothing but pick himself up, stuttering. Cale became the
hero of the school, and he liked the attention. He
continued to harass Jimmy for several weeks, but then
one day Jimmy showed up at school without the cast.
Cale swallowed hard, then hit Jimmy as hard as he
could, not knowing the consequences. One more
punch, and Jimmy went down. Cale jumped on top
of him, and continued to shower punches on Jimmy
until Jimmy no longer resisted. Cale jumped up,
heading for the school, but hesitated. He felt a little
sorry for Jimmy. He decided to go back, reaching out
his hand to help Jimmy up. They shook hands and
immediately became friends. Jimmy was killed in an
auto accident several years later, but Cale still gives
him the credit for helping him build his courage and
confidence today.

The old wooden house became too small for the
family when J.C. was born, so Julian built a new brick
house in town for them to live in. It was nice to have
a new house, with indoor plumbing and central heat. It
was also nice to have close neighbors for the first time.

Oh, sure, everybody knew Cale already, and he knew them, but it felt good to be a part of a community.

Cale heard that the Chevrolet dealer in Darlington, about 15 miles away, would be sponsoring a soap box derby on Labor Day, 1950. He rushed home from school that day and began rummaging through the cotton gin and other farm buildings, compiling materials to construct the fastest soap box derby car in the world. He found some lumber, removed some nails from the barn (he didn't have much of a budget at this time), and finally went to his dad to ask for help getting the required wheels and axles, which had to be purchased from the Chevrolet dealer. The rules stated that he must build the car himself, but Cale knew some of his friends had received more than a little help. Julian made sure that Cale did the work, but he was able to come up with some better building materials and a lot of advice. Cale was stoked! He designed and redesigned the car until he was sure that it would be the best, the fastest, and the one to beat. He painted it white because he had learned from the cowboy movies that good guys always wear white.

Race day arrived, and the family loaded up in the pickup, with Cale, his brothers, and the racer in the

> **He designed and redesigned the car until he was sure that it would be the best, the fastest, and the one to beat.**

bed, and headed for Darlington. By the time they reached town, there was already a crowd assembled for the race. Racers were going over their multicolored creations for the last time, making sure they were ready for the competition. Cale's confidence was unabated; he was sure his was the car to beat, and he already daydreamed about receiving the trophy at the day's end. He had felt the admiration of the crowd and the other competitors in the dream, and even now he was forming a victory speech in his young head. Shortly, the racers were paired off, and the racing began.

Cale would never forget how terrible it felt to lose.

Cale watched the races one by one, with his dad sharing tips to help Cale get the most from his run. "You've got to hold 'er straight," he advised. "Any time you have to steer from side to side, you will lose speed. Remember that."

As the time came to line up at the starting line, Cale tried to recap his preparations. He was ready. When the gate lifted, it seemed to take forever for the car to start rolling. The hills in Darlington are not known as steep. Cale was scrunched down low behind the little windshield, with just the top of his helmet protruding from the cockpit. Movement progressed, the pace quickened, and the wind began to rush past his head as he made a beeline down that hill. What a sensation! It was like nothing he had experienced before. Partway down the hill, Cale noticed the yellow car in the other lane was pulling ahead ever so slightly. The gap continued to widen until the finish line, where Cale had lost by two car lengths. He couldn't believe it. The disappointment overwhelmed him, and tears began to well in his eyes. It seemed as if it took forever for his family to reach him. He stood close to his dad's side. There was little to be said until his dad told him, "You sure did hold it straight, Cale. I don't think I've ever seen anybody drive a car any better." But it was small consolation, for he had lost. Cale would never forget how terrible it felt to lose.

Julian was an attentive dad, proud of his boys. Cale, being the oldest, received the bulk of his dad's attention. By the age of nine, Cale had learned from his dad to drive the pickup through the fields. But one of the greatest influences Julian had on his eldest was his love for stock-car racing. There was, at the time, a dirt racetrack in almost every town of any size, and Julian would take Cale to the races with him. Together, they would travel to Columbia, Florence, and Sumter to watch the races. They would stand at the fence, with their fingers clutching the metal wire, and watch as the warriors on the track would swap positions lap after lap. Cale could see his dad's eyes follow a particular driver around the short track. They would always have a hot dog and a Coke—the dust from the race would cover everything, but the dust only made the hot dogs taste better.

The Yarborough family was a tough family, not to be crossed, but kind and close. They were always there to help each other in times of need. And there had been plenty of those times, as tragedy seemed to haunt them. Julian had lost one brother to a tractor accident and another when a blasting cap detonated prematurely. Grandpa Yarborough had died when Cale was very young, and they never got to know one another. Grandma Yarborough held the family close, though, staying with first one child, then another for a few weeks at a time. Cale and his brothers would look forward to the times when she would come to visit because she would relate the stories of old to them. Sundays were family days, as they would all go to the Sardis Baptist Church, then meet for Grandma's fried chicken dinner at the home where she was staying at the time. It was the best fried chicken they had ever eaten, crispy on the outside and moist inside.

Julian was the athletic sort, known for being able to kick a football a country mile with his bare feet. A daredevil, adventurous spirit led him to be one of the first in the area to take up an interest in flying. He went to the M.B. Huggins Airport in Timmonsville, a grass strip with a couple of Pipers and a few hangars, and took a few lessons. It didn't take long for the bug to bite hard, and he bought his own Piper. He would take it up as often as he could, teaching himself the finer points of flying. Cale would go up with him, looking down at the patchwork of farmland that moved beneath them. The expanse of flat terrain lent itself to sudden changes in weather and thermal drafts that would toss the little plane around, adding to the excitement of the ride. Cale knew that he, like his dad, was destined to fly like an eagle.

The summer of 1950 was the first time Cale was able to attend the Sardis Baptist Church's camp for boys aged 11 to 17 in Aiken, South Carolina. Being so far away from home for the first time, Cale enjoyed the adventure of staying in a cabin, fishing, swimming, and sit-

He could feel his tears begin to flow, and he felt as if his entire body had gone numb.

ting at the nightly bonfires where the counselors would tell ghost stories so real that every sound throughout the night would catch all the boys' attention. But Cale surely missed his family. They had all gone to Myrtle Beach for a vacation while he was away. All went well at camp until Friday night. During the nightly bonfire, he was approached by the camp director, who pulled him aside. The director spoke in a serious tone, different than that used for scolding, but serious, nonetheless, and said he was going to have to take Cale home. He tried to explain to the child that God works in mysterious ways, but that He always has a plan, even if it isn't understood. There had been an accident, and Cale's dad had been killed.

The director continued to speak, but Cale didn't hear a word of it. He could feel his tears begin to flow, and he felt as if his entire body had gone numb. It was a quiet ride home, where the family had already assembled at the house. His relatives all assured him that it would be all right and reminded him that he was now the man of the family. Cale could sense the burden of responsibility. Being a Yarborough, he kept his grief to himself, assuring everyone that he was strong enough to handle whatever tasks were ahead of him. But inside, he wondered to himself how he would be able to do anything without his dad. As time began to pass, there was little talk of Julian's death. There was hardly any time to talk, anyhow, as there were so many chores to do. Thankfully, Jerry was old enough to be of help. And, at night when he was alone, Cale remembered his dad, and many nights his pillow had a damp spot from the tears he privately shed. It was the greatest pain imaginable, but he felt he should keep it hidden.

In the months following, the family struggled to fall into a new routine. In some ways, all seemed fine, but things would never be the same. His mother explained that Julian had made a return flight from Myrtle Beach to check on his businesses and the farm workers, and the plane had crashed into the woods. Nobody witnessed the crash or knew the cause. It had just happened. His mother showed strong resolve, maintaining firm control of the farm and businesses in an era when women rarely ventured into the business world. She hired men to do the heavier jobs, and the general store, the cotton gin, and the farm continued to run smoothly. Cale was truly proud of his mom and extended every effort to help wherever he could. Together, they were determined to keep their lives as close as possible to the way they had been before. But the pain of their loss continued to contribute to sleepless nights and bad dreams for quite a while.

For Cale, the pain only began to dull when he heard again of the soap box derby race, to be held this time in Florence. He immersed himself into racing again, determined to win. He figured aerodynamics was the reason

He knew it was still a few years away, but he determined at that very moment to become a race car driver. He wouldn't lose again.

for his prior loss, so he redesigned the front end of the car and cut down the windshield until it barely existed. He could crouch farther into the cockpit and barely see ahead, but the difference should be sufficient. Doing all the work himself, he enlisted the help of his brothers to push the car for its test runs. When the car was complete, he painted it red, white, and blue, and was ready to race. His uncle Dwight came over to help load the racer into the old pickup, and Dwight, Mom, Cale, and his brothers headed for Florence.

Upon arrival, Cale surveyed the competition and marveled at some of the different shapes and designs others had incorporated into their cars. Some of the cars even had corporate sponsorship, with names and logos adorning the flanks. But Cale's confidence was strong and stable, and he was looking forward to his sure victory. He drew an early starting position and studied his competition. The car he would line up against was one of the fancy cars with sponsorship, but it didn't worry him. At the starting line, he focused on the Chevy logo on the gate until he felt it move from in front of him, and they were off. This time, things were happening a little faster, as the hill had a little more slope than the one in Darlington. Again, the wind rushed around him, and he loved it. He was really moving now, and he could see that the race was pretty much a dead heat. As they passed the finish line, Cale was unsure if he had won or not until he saw the officials running toward the other driver. He had lost again! This time, there were no tears. No, sir, this time Cale was just plain mad. This would be his last soap box derby. Never again would he compete where the driver had so little to do with the outcome of the race. He needed a motor in front of him. He knew it was still a few years away, but he determined at that very moment to become a race car driver. He wouldn't lose again. For the rest of his childhood, life changed for Cale. He adopted a daredevil-type attitude, willing to try almost anything for a thrill. He didn't even realize that he was preparing for his life to come. Nor did he know that this newfound attitude would place him in more strange and dangerous situations than most people ever experience and survive.

About a year and a half after Julian was killed, Annie Mae began seeing a gentleman from Olanta named Vernon Floyd. He visited the Yarborough house frequently, and seemed to be quite a decent fellow. After a short while, the brothers began to realize the relationship between Vernon and their mom was likely to continue. They knew no one could ever take their dad's place, and were unsure of what to expect. So it was no complete surprise when, one day, Mom called a family meeting. She addressed

"I'll never fill your father's shoes, but y'all are fine boys, and I would be proud to be your friend, your brother," he told them.

the boys in a tone reserved for church or other serious times. She explained, "You boys know that Vernon and I have been seeing a lot of each other. And you know we need help on the farm. Even when God brings tragedy into our lives, he means for our lives to go on. Vernon and I are getting married. Vernon will never take the place of your dad, but he can be a friend and companion. And I'd like for you to accept him as that, a friend and a companion, that's all. Can y'all do that for me?" They answered together, "Yes'm," in barely audible tones. Cale wondered if he could do it. Vernon had been waiting on the porch, and Mom went out to get him. He came into the room, took a minute to study each boy, and then he reassured them. "I'll never fill your father's shoes, but y'all are fine boys, and I would be proud to be your friend, your brother," he told them. There was no better way he could have begun the conversation. The boys didn't need a new dad, but they could sure use another brother. Mom had been right about needing the help around the farm, and besides, now Cale would have a big brother, too.

CHAPTER 2

Becoming a Man

Following the immediate shock caused by the loss of his father, Cale became more than aware of a greater sense of responsibility than he'd ever been faced with. He had picked up a stalwart work ethic over the years observing his parents and family, and it seemed to automatically kick in. He and his brother Jerry helped where they could to keep the family farm and other business moving along smoothly. His mother, determined to continue their lifestyle and values, served as an example to Cale and his brothers. Her persistence combined with her energy usually meant that things around the farm stayed pretty busy, leaving little time for grieving and sorrow. Still, there were many times that a particular sound or movement would cause Cale to forget, for a moment, and maybe look up, expecting his dad to be there.

Vernon was about to become a family member now, and the three boys wondered what to expect. Would he be capable of standing beside them as a brother and friend? It turned out that Vernon was completely genuine in his feelings for the boys, and their appreciation for him soon turned to love. Vernon was always there for them, lending counsel and guidance, helping with projects or lessons, and he became woven into the family fabric. It was as if he'd been around forever, but he never threatened to interfere or replace their precious memories of their father, just as he'd promised.

Cale sure was glad to have him around. He could go back to being a boy, spending time with his friends and exploring the world around him. It soon became apparent that whatever they were into at the time, Cale was always the most daring, the most dangerous, and the least cautious of the group. His antics sometimes gained him attention from his peers and others, and he began to relish the spotlight, often seeking opportunities to show off. He often let his mouth react before his brain, but whenever he would consider whatever commitment he'd made, he'd still continue. Backing down wouldn't suit his image, either to his friends or to himself. And besides, it most often would turn out in Cale's favor. However, it did tend to lead to bizarre events, some that are downright hard to believe.

The swamps and marshes in the area were some of the boys' favorite playgrounds. The snakes, alligators, and other wildlife were abundant and ever-present. Today, you can sometimes see a scientist capturing snakes on television. Usually they will place a forked rod behind the snake's head, then reach down care-fully and pick up the animal behind the fork for inspection. Cale and his friends were using forked sticks in the '40s to pick up poisonous copperheads…just for kicks. Some of his friends shied away from this practice, squeamish and cautious, but Cale would pick up more than anyone else. When they would finish with the snakes, they would throw them into the river, competing to see who could throw his snake the farthest.

Cale was always the most daring, the most dangerous, and the least cautious of the group.

One time, right when Cale was beginning to take an interest in girls, he had done some showing off for a particular little beauty named Mary Ann earlier in the day. As he was doing homework that afternoon, he heard her sweet voice calling his name from the front yard. He leapt from his studies and, in his bare feet, burst through the screen door, leaped across the porch, jumped the steps, and landed directly beside a rat-tlesnake. Reacting instantly, Cale jumped again, trying to clear the snake before the animal could react. Too late! As Cale sailed above the snake, it struck his foot, injecting its venom. Cale looked at Mary Ann, excused himself awkwardly, and rushed into the house. He grabbed his pocket knife, cut the bite, and began to suck the poison from his foot, as he'd seen in the movies. His mom rushed in and, realizing the seriousness of the situation, hurried him to the doctor's office. The doctor performed his craft, but the bite made Cale quite sick for a few days. He found, though, that upon his recovery he was lauded as a hero, and the story had changed many times, with the snake getting bigger and bigger, and the conflict between man and beast becoming more and more exciting.

As Cale sailed above the snake, it struck his foot, injecting its venom.

The geography of the area permitted an array of playgrounds for the youngsters year-round. Fishing, hunting, and exploring the swamps and woods became second nature to most already accustomed to the outdoor regimen required of farmers. Summertime always brought tropical heat and humidity, as the temperature typically reaches into the 90s for as long as 30 days in a row and ventures into the low 100s for several days in July and August. Down the road about a mile from Cale's house, there was a bend in the Lynches River that formed the perfect swimming hole. The water was clean and about five feet deep, a perfect place to cool off. The tall trees formed a canopy for protection from the sun's hottest rays. The riverbank was sandy and wide enough to create a sufficient beach area for the boys to congregate. And there was this huge cypress tree growing in the bend at the very edge of the water, reaching straight up—a perfect place to hang a rope swing. They all took their turns swinging out over the swimming hole and flying into the deepest part of the water. One day, Cale grew tired of the swing and suggested that they should build a diving platform in the cypress. The boys rummaged some lumber and nailed a plank into the tree every several feet to form a ladder. At about 30 feet up, Jerry was ready to begin the platform, but Cale kept building the ladder higher and higher. His friend Claude Springs protested as they continued up the tree. Cale finally reached the top of the tree, about 80 feet up, and proceeded to construct a makeshift platform. He called out to the others, "Who's gonna be the first to try it out?"

Claude hollered up, "It's your platform, Cale."

Cale had already known he was to be the first. He stood on the platform, looking down at the water. He picked the spot where he wanted to land, assumed a Tarzan-like pose, and left his lofty perch. He had not given himself enough time to be afraid, but he had not had much time for planning, either. On the way down, he knew that he would have to hit the water at an angle, or else he could bury himself into the sandy bottom. Five feet of water is not a lot to dive into at such velocity. But he plunged perfectly, coming to the surface to the cheers of his friends. Immediately, he climbed right back up that tree to do it again. And again. Each time there was the rush of the wind, the knot in the pit of his stomach, the short burst of adrenaline, and the admiration of those who were there. No one else would ever attempt the dive, but Cale became a master. Heck, word got around, and people passing by in their cars would stop to watch sometimes. Cale sure did love the attention.

One day, on his first dive of the day, Cale brushed into an unfamiliar log at the bottom of the pool when he entered the water. Opening his eyes, he saw that it was not a log but an alligator about eight feet in length. Familiar with alligators, he knew that he needed to hold its mouth shut, as an alligator's strength is in its clamping down but the muscles it uses to open its mouth are somewhat weak. He held the gator's head under his arm as they thrashed around in the water. Too far from the shore to escape, Cale held on for dear life. The gator rolled over and over, giving Cale the ride of his life. Somehow, they rolled nearer the shore, and Cale felt his feet hit the bottom. He yelled to the others to grab sticks and beat the animal in hopes of scaring it enough to help it forget about making lunch plans. Now that he had firmer footing, he thrust the gator away from his body. The gator must have been as scared and surprised as Cale was, because it headed away as quickly as it could go. What a relief! Cale checked himself and found everything in order,

He picked the spot where he wanted to land, assumed a Tarzan-like pose, and left his lofty perch.

although he looked like he had been caught in the middle of a briar patch, with scratches all over him. Wrestling alligators would never find its way into Cale's ambitions, but what a story to tell! And he had witnesses to verify that it was the truth. The only problem was keeping the story from his mother because he knew if she heard it, he was likely never to see the swimming hole again.

Cale survived another scare during a summertime thunderstorm, a common occurrence in South Carolina. Cale had spent many days studying the cloud formations and wind patterns that accompany the spontaneous

Opening his eyes, he saw that it was not a log but an alligator about eight feet in length.

bursts of lightning in the skies above. Sometimes the thunder would begin as a dull roar in the distance, then build into a full crescendo as the sound moved closer and closer. The lightning would sometimes come from behind the billowing and ominous clouds, framing them in light and showing for a brief moment the outline of the storm. At other times, the lightning streaks would spread from horizon to horizon, flashing and displaying awesome power. During one of these storms, Cale stood in amazement at the window in their living room. It seemed that the lightning was battling itself in the sky, with streaks forming in all directions and stretching into and away from each other. He had watched storms many times, so he was not afraid, but he thought that this just might qualify as the best light show he had ever seen. Suddenly, a fireball hit the ground near the house, and Cale watched it as it raced toward the window. The next thing he could remember was waking up next to the television on the other side of the room. He checked himself out, wiggled his fingers and toes, then stood up and looked around. The whole room was a mess, the window shattered inward, and the wind and commotion, combined with Cale's flight across the room, had knocked things around. But, to his surprise, he was intact and seemed no worse for the wear. Cale began to feel like Captain Marvel. He had been struck by lightning and not only survived, but wasn't even hurt.

Cale began to feel like Captain Marvel. He had been struck by lightning and not only survived, but wasn't even hurt.

There had always been an old Indian motorcycle in the barn, and Cale had ridden it around the farmyards since he was tall enough to reach the pedals. He had grown bored with it, though, and it had been sitting for quite a while. One day, he and his brothers decided to start it up so he could learn to do some trick riding. Jerry, J.C., and Cale pushed it outside, cleaned it up, and proceeded to try to start it. It was a big bike, with a huge, heavy kick-starter.

Try as they might, the boys couldn't get the bike to fire up. They took turns kicking and kicking, but none was of great enough size to turn the engine over with authority. Thankfully, Vernon had been keeping an eye on the boys and came to see if he could help them. He suggested that maybe they should check the spark plugs to see if they were dirty. Sure enough, Vernon was right, so they all hopped in the pickup for a ride to the local filling station. The garage had a spark plug blast cleaner, so the job took just a few minutes. When they returned to the farm, they installed the plugs, and to their surprise, the old bike fired up. Over the next weeks, much of Cale's time was spent astride the old Indian. He was not allowed to ride it on the road, which was probably a very good thing. Falling in the sand was treacherous enough, and falling was not uncommon, as Cale had now taken to jumping the motorcycle over ditches and mounds around the fields. The jumping required a keenness and control that quickly developed, and before long there were many more good jumps than bad. It became great fun and expanded further when Cale would get in the old pickup and put it through some of the same paces expected of the bike. Jumping the truck was a blast, and when he would land, he would have to be careful not to hit his head on the roof as he bounced around the cab. His playtimes were gravitating more toward the mechanical, setting precedents not yet realized.

In September of 1953, Cale was enrolled as a freshman at Timmonsville High School. When his bus arrived at school on the first day, he ran straight to the gym where he found the football coach, Wallace Walkup. "I'm ready to play, Coach. Where's my uniform?" he said. Truth is, if Cale had been allowed, he would have joined the team even before he reached high school. The coach replied, "Cale, I believe they are looking for you in homeroom. We'll look forward to seeing you later when we have practice. We'll pass out the uniforms then. So, why don't you head along now." Cale was crushed. He had hoped that high school would be more about sports and girls, in that order, and less about studying. But he could see that he was wrong. He was quite glad that he could get by with studying less than most. Now all he had to do was become a big football star so he could attract all the girls. He wasn't worried that he stood only 5'5" and 135 pounds. Timmonsville was a small school, and only 15 boys joined the football team. Cale was sure that he would see action, maybe even have a chance to play in the starting lineup. If sheer determination and trying hard had anything to do with it, it was certain to happen.

At practice, Coach Walkup welcomed the boys and showed them a pile of old pads and uniforms to pick through to find their sizes. Cale chose the best he could find and headed toward the locker room. The coach had told them to pick out a locker, get dressed, and meet him on the field. The old locker room, painted in institutional beige, vibrated with the sounds of the steel locker doors clanging shut and the excited conversations of the soon-to-be warriors. There was a musty odor of sweat, old uniforms, and years of competition in the air. Cale was one of the first to emerge onto the field, and he stood there for a minute, soaking up a full view of the field, the goalposts, and the bleachers on each side. In his mind's eye he could see himself sprinting down the sideline into the end zone for a touchdown with the voice of the announcer blasting from the speakers: "And there he goes again, folks! The Timmonsville Flash has scored one more time!" The coach blew his whistle, and Cale returned to reality.

"Boys, we are a small team," Coach started. "We don't even have enough boys to form a scrimmage game between ourselves. So we are going to get in the best shape possible. We cannot afford to get hurt, and there's less of a chance of getting hurt if we are in good shape. That means no smoking, no drinking pop, and no abusing yourselves, if you know what I mean. We are going to work hard every day so any of you will be able to play 60 minutes of any game. It's all up to you."

Cale knew that at his size the only way for him to succeed was by being tough. So he took what the coach had said to heart, and vowed to get and stay in the best shape he could. Even today, at age 68, he maintains a fit and chiseled physique.

The coach had them all form a line and run 100-yard wind sprints from one end of the field to the other. On the first trip down, Cale found that he was fastest of them all, easily crossing into the end zone before the others. On the next sprint he found that it took longer for him to get a lead, but he could still outpace the field. The coach had noticed also. "Hey, Cale," he said. "Nice job. You're pretty fast. On the next race, why don't you line up five yards behind them and see if you can still win?" As Cale lined up, he was sure that he could still win. At about 50 yards, a pain shot through his side, but he still passed the last boy with about 20 yards left and won going away. "All right! Now let's see if you can do it from 10 yards back," Coach yelled. Cale thought, *He must be kidding,* as he lined up 10 yards back. His side already hurt, his legs were beginning to burn, but he still expected to win. He just hoped this would be the last race. Ten yards is a lot of ground to make up in a 100-yard race, but Cale's legs churned, gaining ground little by little. He managed to catch the last boy right at the end line and won the race by, literally, a nose. He fell into the end zone, exhausted. He got up and moved slowly towards the locker room, making sure he would be the last one in. When everyone had entered the building, he promptly threw up.

> **"I'm ready to play, Coach. Where's my uniform?" he said.**

The team practiced dutifully in preparation of their first game, a home stand against the Lamar High School team. Thankfully, Lamar was one of the few schools in their conference that was as small as they were. Cale had earned the spot as the starting full-back, and butterflies danced in his stomach as the team readied itself for the field. The team played well, earning a win in a contest where Cale's speed served him well. He had scored his first touchdown, an end around from the 15-yard line, in front of the home crowd. The cheering and accolades were sweet music to his ears. The pats on the back helped to complete a feeling of success and excellence. Cale imagined that this must be how it would have been if he had won the soap box derby in Florence two years earlier. He had yearned for this feeling, and now he had finally experienced it.

His freshman season continued to go well, with Timmonsville winning more than half of their games. Playing fullback on offense and linebacker on defense, Cale played every minute of every game the entire season. Sports, especially football, began to dominate Cale's life. He kept himself in the best possible shape year-round. He didn't ever want to experience "first day's pain" the way he did his freshman season. He played baseball and basketball, keeping busy most of the year, but his passion was football. He counted down the days until school started. By his sophomore and junior years, the team had grown in size and reputation. Building successive winning records, they gained respect from their rivals. Even though they were one of the smaller schools, they began to be known as giant-killers. Cale's confidence and determination made him the team leader, known now as the "Timmonsville Flash." He was beginning to get used to the attention of success, and it fit him like a soft leather glove. However, something in his life was coming that football would have to share time with.

March 27, 1953, finally arrived. Cale had been dreaming of this day forever. That was the day Cale could legally begin driving. It was his 14th birthday. He awoke before dawn, waking his brothers and the rest of the house as well. "Happy Birthday, Cale," chimed Mama and Vernon as he reached the kitchen. "It's so hard to believe you are already 14 years old. So, what do you want to do today?" they mused. "I want to get my driver's license, that's what I want to do today!" It was more blurted out in exasperation than normally spoken. What else could he have possibly wanted to do? The whole family had a good laugh, with Mom replying, "Calm down, Cale, we oughta be able to go to Florence after school today and get your learner's permit." After school seemed far too distant. "How about we go at lunchtime, Mama?" But her final answer was, "Oh, I believe we can wait 'til after school. We'll pick you up out front." It was probably the longest school day ever, but he made it through and finally got his permit later that afternoon.

Cale studied his driver's booklet harder than he had even studied his football playbook. He had his friends test him until he could answer every question perfectly. He learned every nuance, all the signs, signals, and rules of the road. He was really feeling good about passing the test until his friend Russell DeFee asked him, "Do you know how to park?" Parking was a foreign concept to Cale. He wasn't going to be parking; he was going to be driving. "You don't think you can just drive around the block and they'll hand you your license, do you? You'll have to parallel park, too, or they won't let you have it," Russell informed him. So he went home, laid out a parking course using some old kegs from the store, and proceeded to practice parking the family car, a 1951 Buick. Vernon came home to find the kegs all broken and splintered. He slid into the passenger seat and offered some advice: "Slow down, Cale. There's no hurry. Just ease back and up, placing the car just where you want it." Slowing down caused the task to become much easier, and before the evening was over, Cale had mastered the art of parallel parking to the point he was sure he could get a job as a parking lot attendant. The next Thursday, he passed the test and received his driver's license. Now, all he needed was a car.

He found himself a part-time job at Gregory's Tobacco Warehouse after school and began to scour the area for a car he could afford. There wasn't nearly enough time to save up the kind of money needed for a new car, so he decided he'd look for something cheap he could get soon. He could fix it up while he drove it, and felt sure he could repair anything that might break. It didn't take long before he ran across an old 1930 Ford Model A coupe. It was only $75, but there were reasons it was so affordable. The old car was rough—the fenders were bent, the top was dented in, the front bumper was missing, glass was broken, and the paint had long since lost its protection qualities. At least it ran well, and, besides, Cale planned to strip the car anyway. Removing the unwanted parts required a lot of penetrating oil and some extra elbow grease, but soon the old Ford looked like a hot rod. Cale took a hacksaw to the roof and removed it completely. The fenders and bumpers were removed, and he painted it shiny red. The addition of lowering blocks and a Smitty's muffler completed the package. As the summer passed, Cale anticipated his junior year of high school. He knew football was coming up soon, so he saved all he could for gas money. He would not be able to keep his job at Gregory's during the season, and he was surely going to need his car. The girls were going to love it.

Seventy-five dollar hot rods have frequent needs, especially when driven with the accelerator mashed to the floor and when slid into parking lots sideways most every time. So money always was in short supply. It didn't stop Cale from enjoying the social life of a high school star jock. There were two drive-ins in Timmonsville, and all the kids hung out there on the weekends. Cale and the rod were regulars, and there were always guys hanging around, talking cars and racing. They would talk of ways to make their cars faster and search the boneyards for special parts to one-up each other. Cale would buy himself a milk shake and make it last all night to save money. The talk would sometimes lead to street racing out on Highway 403 where it branched off Highway 76. It was two lanes, and the pavement was in pretty good shape with a six mile stretch that led straight into Sardis. The long, flat straight allowed you to see any oncoming traffic a mile off, two miles at night when you could see the oncoming headlights in the distance. It made for a perfect place to wind out the old cars and see who was the fastest this week. Speeds steadily increased as each boy would find a new trick or be able to install a new performance part to his ride. And always, when the racing was over, they would return to the drive-in to talk more racing.

After football season, Cale went back to work at Gregory's. By the time he was ready to begin his senior year, he was able to purchase a used 1955 Ford convertible with a big V8. He added a hotter camshaft, a larger carb, free-flow exhaust, and a high-speed rear end, and the Ford became the scourge of the Highway 403 drag strip. He was able to whip all comers until some local fellow built an Olds 88 that could take him.

Football season was coming fast, and the season looked a little different for the boys from Timmonsville. This year they were lauded as the team to beat. There was even talk of a state championship. Coach Walkup and the entire team could feel the increased pressure to perform, and as the first practices of the year began, they vowed to work harder than ever before. The local sportswriters filled the newspapers and radio broadcasts with glorious previews of the upcoming season. And, of course, Cale was expected to make the All-State team easily. This was the most attention Timmonsville had ever been given, and they were proud to be in the spotlight. At season's end, they were picked to play Summerville for the championship of the Lower State. Cale and the other players couldn't even walk down the street without someone wishing them well and telling them how good they were. The entire town was behind them. It would be the biggest game ever.

Game time arrived, and the team was pumped. Coach Walkup offered a stirring speech that whipped them into a frenzy, and they stormed onto the playing field like a bunch of wild men. Even though they were picked as the underdog, they were utterly convinced they would be victorious. The whole town must have been at the game, with signs and banners and applause that aroused the butterflies in each of the players' stomachs. Then Summerville took the field. They were huge. And the roar from the crowd was deafening. The cheers Timmonsville had enjoyed now seemed only a whimper in contrast. The overall confidence and enthusiasm of the Timmonsville team waned for a moment, then both teams assembled in the middle of the field for the coin toss. Timmonsville won the toss and chose to receive. Then they returned to their respective locker rooms for their final pep talk from the coaches before the game. Coach Walkup was able to return the team to their original fervor by expressing his faith in their ability to do their best. He assured them that if they could strike first, they could take some wind from Summerville's sails. So

"We gotta make sure to get the ball to Cale, no matter what. And Cale, you gotta run like the wind."

his final instructions were, "We gotta make sure to get the ball to Cale, no matter what. And Cale, you gotta run like the wind. Boys, we need this one, so let's go." Timmonsville returned to the field with a renewed vitality, ready to make their mark.

The football sailed through the air straight to Ramsey Mallette, who was waiting on the 5-yard line. Mallette secured the kick and headed in Cale's direction. The lateral was completed on the 15, and Cale sprinted toward the left sideline. He could hear, even feel, the approaching defenders on his heels. He knew these were the fastest members of the Summerville team, and if he could elude their charge, he would have a chance for a big play. Just as they lunged toward him, he turned, faked, and headed diagonally toward the sideline. The fake caught all the defenders off guard, and Cale found a clear field all the way to the end zone 85 yards away. The crowd noise was deafening, and Cale imagined that this was finally the applause he had expected way back when had competed in the soap box derby. Finally, he could enjoy the feeling of triumph. Then he saw the yellow flag flying slowly through the air, signaling that a foul had been committed. A clipping penalty was being called against Timmonsville, so the touchdown wouldn't count. On the next kickoff, the team couldn't get the ball to Cale, and the rest of the game followed suit. Timmonsville was never really in the game and lost by two touchdowns. Still, the team is remembered as the best ever fielded by Timmonsville High School.

In the off-season, Cale took up boxing, competing in the Golden Gloves competition in the welterweight division. He displayed his usual tenacity and enthusiasm, studying the sweet science and progressing in his abilities. Golden Glove boxing was pretty popular, and most towns fielded a team of hopefuls. During his senior year, Cale became state champion. He had worked long and hard for the honor, but he really had wanted to win that football game.

With the sports seasons behind him, Cale's attention was, of course, drawn back to stock-car racing. His days as a spectator were numbered—further involvement seemed a certainty. Bobby and Irby Weatherly had begun a team called Palmetto Racing, and Cale became a crew member. He even had a red jacket with "Palmetto Racing" and his name embroidered on it. He didn't get paid, but now he was an official crew member and a part of the action. This was much better than being a spectator. He soaked up the atmosphere, and racing began to become a part of him. There seemed no doubt that, in some capacity, Cale was destined to make his mark at the racetrack. If this was to be his destiny, Cale was, once again, going to be Cale—he would set his goals high. Cale was determined to make it all the way to NASCAR.

> There seemed no doubt that, in some capacity, Cale was destined to make his mark at the racetrack.

Bobby Weatherly was a very important figure in the evolution of stock-car racing in the area. He owned some grading equipment and built several dirt racetracks. Tracks in Hemingway, Ashwood, Sumter, and Darlington were all of his design and construction. All of these local tracks would hold weekly events, entertaining many locals. These tracks were called "outlaw tracks" because they had no uniform rules structures. Some were "run what you brung"–type tracks, where you could race anything as long as you had rudimentary safety equipment and a will to compete. With so many tracks so close to home, Cale was itching to have his own race car.

Once again, Cale went back to work at Gregory's and began looking around to find a car suitable for the track. It would have to be a special car, one that he could afford. The search included all the places where old cars hide—barns, behind buildings, the back of used car lots, and the local junkyards provided ample opportunities. Finally, behind the Ford dealership in Timmonsville, Cale found a 1935 Ford up on blocks. It ran, and the body wasn't too bad. Fifty dollars later, the old Ford was being towed to the warehouse, where it would start its new life as a race car. Cale enlisted Ashton Phillips and his cousin Lynwood to help in the process, and a race team was born. Transforming the old Ford into a racer was simple enough. Some used pipe was found to form a roll bar, and the car was gutted. All of the glass and interior was removed. Door panels, insulation, headliner, and any other component not necessary for performance were discarded. The army surplus store supplied some four-inch-wide seatbelts. The team was very careful to form the roll bar to offer the most protection. They secured the seatbelts to the frame of the car, sure that, at some time or another, the car would probably end up on its roof. The drivetrain and suspension modifications needed were beyond the team's experience and knowledge, so they would tow the car from place to place, receiving advice and assistance. Building a race car takes time, especially when you are still in high school, working a job after school, and still trying to maintain some sort of social life. Weeks passed. It would sure have been nice for Cale to be able to buy a bigger V8 from a truck, but finances dictated patching up the old flat-head. There was enough money for some firmer springs and such, but it didn't make a whole lot of sense to spend a fortune on a car that, even on a winning night, could only win $25 or so. The finishing touches included a white paint job and the number 35 painted on the door. The number had been good to Cale in football, so why not in racing, too? Now they were ready to go.

There was a quarter-mile track in Sumter that held racing each Saturday night with no restrictions. Definitely a "run what you brung"–type of track, where you might find yourself lined up beside any kind of car. Your closest opponent might have driven his family to the race in the car he was racing. Or it could be a purpose-built racer that could blow your doors off. You wouldn't know until the race began. Cale, Ashton, and Lynwood fashioned a tow bar for the Ford convertible, hooked up the race car, and headed for Sumter. The trip to Sumter seemed to last twice as long as usual, and, even though there was some excited conversation along the way, for the most part they sat in the car wide-eyed and quiet in anticipation of their first race. There was already activity at the track when they arrived, and finding a suitable place to park in the infield proved to be a task. After all, infield space at a quarter-mile track is limited, and there was a fair turnout of locals vying for a chance to race. An appropriate spot on the backstretch became their pit area, with enough room to ready the car for the night's activities. Now it was time to start the car and find out just what they had built. Cale climbed into the car, buckled his army surplus belt, pulled his helmet on, and fired it up. The engine sounded good, and Cale was quite comfortable in the cockpit. He checked the few gauges in the old Ford, then glanced at the fourth turn to survey the action already happening on the dirt oval.

What was he supposed to do now? Just as it was when he had built the platform 80 feet above the Lynches River, Cale had never really considered what was next. He had spent many Saturday nights standing at the fence watching the action, but he had never considered just what it was he was supposed to do as a driver to ready himself for a race. Oh well, he would just pull out onto the track and watch what the others were doing. If they could do it, so could he. He reached for the shifter, pulled it down into low gear, released the clutch, and moved out onto the racing surface. He found the clay surface afforded more traction than the old country roads he was used to. As he moved around the track, cars were passing him on the left and right. He reached the front straightaway and mashed the throttle to the floor. The first turn came up on him in a hurry, and he cocked the wheels to the left. The old Ford's rear end began to slide around to the right side, so Cale corrected. He drifted through Turns 1 and 2, reaching the backstretch and nailing it again. This was going to be easy, he thought. Entering Turns 3 and 4, he once again jerked the wheel to the left. The rear end swung out again, but this time it didn't stop. It swung the car in a circle, and Cale found himself facing the wrong way, with cars flying by on both sides. *How embarrassing*, he thought. In a flash, he turned around and continued to practice. He remembered how Vernon had taught him to parallel park, deciding to take it a little slower, feel it out, then add speed a little at a time. Practice time was over, so all the racers pulled their cars back into the infield to await their turns at qualifying. At least Cale had learned his way around the track, so he was ready to go.

Qualifying was rather uneventful. Cale turned in a time that was mid-pack, allowing him to start in the fifth position of the eight cars in his first heat race. His strategy would be simple. He would take it easy for the first few laps, noting which cars he would have to race, and which to stay away from. Then he would give it all he had, pass them all, and win the race. It never occurred to him that he had a chance of losing. He was confident in his abilities to build a good car and to drive it.

They lined up for the start, and just as the marshal started to drop the flag, two cars shot by Cale as if they had been shot from a cannon. As he reached the first turn, he jerked the wheel left to put the car into a slide, but the rear wouldn't swing out. Three wide through the turn would not allow room, and metal scraped metal as the cars challenged each other for track position. A caution flag flew as the outside car hit the fence and rolled over on its side. Cale had never had so much fun in his life. The car coming off the fence rolled in front of one of the other cars, causing a collision. The officials just pushed both of the wrecked racers into the infield, and the green flag waved again. This time Cale watched the flagman, and floored it as the flag went up. One car still flew by, but he was getting better. How early would he have to start to get a jump on these guys? It became quite obvious that his original plan was not going to work. Every time he would throw the car into a turn, there was always another car there, and the ensuing contact would interrupt the slide. It reminded Cale of the bumper cars at the carnival. He stayed so busy behind the wheel that time passed quickly, and before he knew it the race was over. He had finished third, with

A caution flag flew as the outside car hit the fence and rolled over on its side. Cale had never had so much fun in his life.

his car still in one piece, even though it did not look like the pretty white car he had brought to the track. It looked more like the old beat-up Ford he had begun with. Finishing third might seem like a pretty good start, but there were only three cars that finished the race. At least he was one of them.

As the night progressed, Cale became more and more familiar with his car and the track. His car was underpowered compared to many of the others, but he learned to use that to his advantage, holding his lines into the corners longer than the others and maneuvering through the traffic skillfully, passing when he could. Handling the loose car began to become second nature to him as he tossed it around the surface, trying to find the best angle to enter and exit each turn.

It didn't take many weeks of racing to convince him that he had a talent for driving. Then he began to feel that he could handle more power. But the Ford wouldn't produce more power without spending more and more money on it, and Cale's income was somewhat limited. He was still in high school and could only work afternoons. So he began showing up at the track and looking for car owners who might need drivers. He would walk through the pits, and when he would see that someone was not getting the most from their car, he would ask if he could have a chance behind the wheel. Weeks passed without any luck. Cale was convinced that he could win races if he had the right car. But he couldn't seem to get into the right car without having won any races. It was a dilemma he would have to solve—the quicker the better. He still campaigned the '35, but it just did not have the power to beat some of the others that showed up each week.

Several weeks later he had just arrived at the Sumter track when there was a multicar pileup on the front stretch. One car ended up on its roof, and the driver emerged from the car and exclaimed, "I quit. I want no more of this!" Cale hurried to the pits, asking whose car that might be. It looked to be a pretty good piece, with a big V8 and the right setup. He quickly found that the car belonged to J.N. Wilson, a respected car builder. With complete confidence, he marched straight over to the car owner, announced himself as the driver of the #35 car, and asked if he might need a new driver for his car. To his surprise, the owner accepted, arranging for next week's ride at the same track. Things were suddenly looking up. This car was competitive and could allow Cale to showcase the skills he was so sure of.

Cale spent some time at J.N.'s race shop in Camden that week and gained respect for both J.N. and the car. It really was a well-built racer with quality new parts. Cale qualified third for their first race together, but he found the wall early in the feature race and languished back in the field for the 15 lapper. For the first time, he really began thinking like a racer, considering the circumstances before making his moves. His potential was obvious to J.N., and a sort of partnership was formed. Each week, Cale improved his standings until, some weeks later, everything came together and he got his first win. It was just a heat race, but the win paid $15. He had to split it with Wilson, but it was still a payday. He was now a professional race car driver. Not bad for a high school senior. Cale had just climbed one more rung on the ladder toward his goal of becoming a NASCAR driver. Cale was beginning to build quite a résumé, and surely his senior yearbook would be filled with accolades. Captain of the football team, all-state, baseball, basketball, boxing, glee club, student council, bus driver, and professional race car driver made the list of accomplishments he amassed. Always involved and busy as a bee, he still found time to race the car at many of the local tracks, occasionally winning. All along, he remained a regular guy, enjoying what could be called an active social life.

One night, Cale and his friend Wallace Jordan invited a couple of girls for hamburgers at the drive-in. Everybody was having a good time until a man standing under the street light wearing a trench coat flashed himself to the girls. Enraged, Cale approached the man, who was obviously quite drunk, and accosted him. "Hey, buddy," Cale said, "you shouldn't do that. You should be ashamed of yourself. There are girls around here." The man shot back, "Of course there are girls around here. You don't think I was flashing you, do you?" As Cale began to walk away, not wanting to cause trouble, the man pulled a gun. "Why don't you put that thing away and leave?" Cale implored as he reached for the weapon. "You don't want to cause any trouble." As Cale touched the gun, it fired a bullet into the pavement. It scared Cale, and it must have scared the man even more because he turned and ran.

"Boy, you're lucky you didn't get shot, Cale," they told him. Then they looked down at his cowboy boot and noticed the blood oozing onto the ground.

The other guys at the drive-in came running as soon as the sound of the gunshot was heard. They huddled around Cale, each wondering what had happened. "Boy, you're lucky you didn't get shot, Cale," they told him. Then they looked down at his cowboy boot and noticed the blood oozing onto the ground. He had been shot! They removed the boot and sock and saw that the bullet had entered between his big and second toes, just grazing the skin. Barely hurt, now he had a ruined cowboy boot to add to his collection of conversation pieces.

Another event occurred during his senior year that helped to form Cale's character. A friend called one day to ask him a favor.

"I have a girlfriend who would really like for you to take her to the prom," she said.

"Well, then, why doesn't she say something to me herself?" Cale asked.

"Because she's afraid you'll say no, and she doesn't want to hear it from you. You see, she had polio when she was young, and she's crippled," she explained.

"Well, I'll have to think about it and get back to you," was Cale's answer.

He thought about it for a couple of days before he called her back. He wondered how his buddies would react to him bringing a disabled girl to the dance. He worried that it would affect his BMOC status. He was afraid he would be looked down on. So he called back to tell his friend he was declining the offer. "That's why she didn't want to ask you her-self," his friend replied. "She admires you too much to bear the disappointment she knew would happen." The phone fell silent for a minute as Cale realized he may have made a mistake. Guilt probably played a part, as well. "Okay, I'll take her to the prom," he blurted as his mind was spinning with thoughts of the possible consequences. He arrived at the girl's house on prom night without expectations. Her mother went to get her, and she came into the room on her aluminum crutches, a little unsteady. She was cute but he still worried about what his buddies would think. Cale helped her to the car, and they headed for the dance. When they arrived, they had to walk down an aisle formed by the tables, and Cale could feel eyes falling on them. For some reason, his fear turned to pride, and by the time they had traversed the aisle, he knew he had made the right decision. The night turned out to be quite a fun time. Cale and the girl danced together, and before the night was over, every other couple at the dance had come to sit at their table and chat. As the night progressed, Cale realized just how fortunate he had been. He had always wished his family had more money and more and better things, but his date that night knew true hardship. He would never entertain those thoughts again.

Graduation came on a Friday night in late May 1957. Of course, there was also a race that night, and he considered missing the ceremony for the race. This time his mother interfered. "William Caleb Yarborough, if you think you are going to deny me the thrill of seeing my first child graduate from high school, you've got another thing coming," she told him. So, there he was, crossing the stage in his white sport jacket. He received his diploma and continued his promenade to the other end of the stage. However, instead of turning left with the other graduates, he turned right, ran to the parking lot, and hurried to the track. He was late, but J.N. was there, and the car was ready to go. Cale jumped in, strapped up, pulled his helmet on, and headed for the track. "You might be late, but you're the best-dressed driver in the field tonight," J.N. told Cale as he readied himself for the night's activities. He joined the others on the track, and promptly went out and won his heat race. He did remove his white jacket before the main event and led most of the race before being spun out with just a couple of laps to go. It may have been the most exciting graduation night of all time—the kind of night movies are written about—had he won the race.

One of the greatest reasons for Cale's early confidence and success was the support of his family. His dad had taught him early that he should never avoid trying something just because it may seem impossible. His mother and Vernon had both consistently encouraged him to accept the challenges he encountered. Of course, they never encouraged him to be dangerous. He seemed able to do that on his own.

CHAPTER 3

Becoming a Racer

During this period in the South, stock-car racing ranked down there with cockfighting, anything that had to do with alcohol, and playing hillbilly music as an acceptable occupation. The fact that the local tracks were called "outlaw" tracks gives an indication of the social standing the sport enjoyed. Most races paid little more than travel money, and sometimes promoters were reluctant to even part with that much. More than once, when it came time to pay up, the promoter would be nowhere to be found.

With high school behind him, Cale had more time for the racetrack. He had made up his mind years ago which course he wanted his life to take. And there had been nothing to change that course. He was gaining consistency in the race car, and, by now, had been accepted into the racing community. Possessing a maturity beyond his years, he began to view racing in new ways. His confidence had fueled his aggression, but often led to trouble. Too often, Cale found himself spun out or in the wall as he fought to find the

front of the pack. There was always only one acceptable position on the track, and that was to be in the
lead. No matter where in the field he started, he headed
toward the front as hard as his car would take him. In
a natural course of development, Cale viewed the field
in front of him with greater clarity. As a direct result,
he could better choose a path forward, exercising a
little patience without losing urgency. He definitely
had a knack for this sport called stock-car racing,
that's for sure.

His talent must have been obvious from his earliest days. J.N. Wilson had certainly recognized it right
off. And his family must have seen it also because they
continued to encourage him. His mother would go
to most of his races, riding to the track with Cale, all
the while trying to get him to slow down. "If you'll
get me home safe, I'll never go with you again," she
would tell him. But the next week she would be ready
and waiting to go to the track. If she couldn't go,
most times Vernon would make the trip, unless the
track was too far away. Then he would wait up for
Cale to get home so they could discuss the night's
event. He was always there to celebrate any victories
or console any losses. Their discussions helped to
sharpen Cale's focus, displacing any doubts with
more confidence in his own abilities.

Timing is often an integral part of any success
story, and this one is no different. The South, as a
whole, had enjoyed little in the way of entertainment

since the Civil War. Most places, especially the small communities like those around central South Carolina, were focused on farming or textile mills and all the related work involved. Excitement was a rare commodity. Growing the largest watermelon in town could constitute a neighborhood event. But stock-car racing offered new opportunities for fun and entertainment. Some of the drivers, like Curtis Turner and Little Joe Weatherly, were racing at the local tracks. Stories of their extraordinary exploits and questionable character were quick to spread, and the crowds at the tracks grew. Cale felt that he could ride their coattails all the way to NASCAR, and began competing at those same tracks. He was making a name for himself among the locals, enough so that, when he announced that he was going to race at Darlington, Bobby Weatherly took up a collection to help buy Cale a new car to race there. However, there was one problem—NASCAR's rules called for a minimum age of 21, and Cale was only 18. But Cale knew a girl down at the courthouse and was able to get her to fill out a phony birth certificate for him. He mailed it in with his application and $5, and received his first NASCAR license in the mail a few days later. He was so proud of it he had it laminated, and still has it

> There was always only one acceptable position on the track, and that was to be in the lead.

today. Bobby went down to White Pontiac with the donations to make a deal on some kind of car they could race at Darlington. They did not have nearly enough money to buy a new one, but White Pontiac joined in to help, providing a brand-new 1957 Pontiac. Now armed with a license and a car, Cale anticipated his first NASCAR run.

NASCAR's rules called for a minimum age of 21, and Cale was only 18. But Cale knew a girl down at the courthouse and was able to get her to fill out a phony birth certificate for him.

NASCAR rules for 1957 limited the modifications that could be made to the cars. They were really to remain stock cars. Some minor engine tuning, beefed-up suspension, a bigger radiator, and an exhaust system were allowed. Interiors were removed, along with the side window glasses and headlights. A roll bar had to be installed for safety, as did seat belts. Firestone and Goodyear had just begun manufacturing stock-car tires the year before. Cale and Bobby went to Thompson Oil Co., the local Goodyear distributor, and were able to get tires for promotion. Money reserves were low, but the local junkyards helped with suspension parts needed. A local sign painter painted a large 30 on both front doors. Cale's usual #35 was already being used in NASCAR by Bill

Champion, so he picked 30 from those numbers available. White Pontiac allowed access to their parts bins and replaced any questionable parts under an informal warranty program. Cale and Bobby were able to compare different engine parts for flaws and weight, winding up with as close to a balanced drivetrain as possible without a machine shop. The white Pontiac was ready a full two weeks before the Darlington race. There was time to run the car up and down Highway 403 to break it in and test the reliability of their build. After each run, they would examine the car for weakness and operation, making adjustments where necessary. Knowing that the top cars would be in the race, but feeling absolute confidence in their car, they were able to improve the car's performance by 30 mph during these test runs.

On the day before the race, a letter arrived from NASCAR. They had discovered Cale's subterfuge about his age and wanted their license back. He discussed the situation with Bobby, and they decided to act as if there had never been a letter. Ignorance is bliss. Besides, the car could always be entered in Bobby's name, as he had a valid NASCAR license. So, they loaded Bobby's pickup with their spare parts, Cale climbed into the Pontiac, and they made their way to the track. It wasn't totally uncommon in those days to drive the car to the race. Butterflies filled his gut as he sped along the long, straight roads that were so familiar. For the first time, he enjoyed the sights along the way. He tried hard to not think about the race, his insides were in such turmoil. This was certainly going to be the biggest challenge he had ever faced, and he knew it. The best race car drivers in the world were going to be at the track, and he was going to get to race against them, finally. His heroes would be there—Lee Petty, Fireball Roberts, Fonty Flock, Speedy Thompson, and Joe Weatherly would be lined up side by side, and he would be lined up with them. Cale knew the task would be formidable, but he was confident in his talent and in his equipment. He was also spurred on by the fact that so many of his neighbors and friends were counting on him to do his dead-level best.

> **His heroes would be there—Lee Petty, Fireball Roberts, Fonty Flock, Speedy Thompson, and Joe Weatherly would be lined up side by side, and he would be lined up with them.**

Having reached the track, they followed the signs to the pits and settled in. All was well until Bobby and Cale went to the official's desk to sign in. "So, who's going to be driving the car?" the official asked. The boys knew the reason for the question, so Bobby answered, "I am." The official responded, "Okay, but make sure he stays out of the car, he's too young." Bobby reassured the official that he would be driving the car, so the appropriate forms were completed, and they were in the race. Cale was absolutely furious! He accosted Bobby as they walked back to their pit, "What do you mean, telling him that?" Bobby explained that he had a plan to switch drivers at the right times, and Cale could still be the driver. Heck, with a helmet and goggles on, who would know? Realizing that his choices were few, Cale agreed and paced impatiently as Bobby took the car out for practice. He even explained his dilemma to several other drivers while he was waiting, and they all told him they didn't care how old he was, as long as he didn't cause them problems on the track. Cale was satisfied that the plan was not to going to be a problem in any other way other than he was going to be hard for them to catch. Bobby came off the track, and Cale asked him, "How is the track? How is she running?" Bobby answered his questions as he climbed from the car. "The car is running just fine. There is a flat spot in Turn 1. And this track is huge." Cale looked around to see if any of the officials were watching and, thinking the coast was clear, he tumbled into the car, strapped in, and headed for the track. His first lap was taken at slow speed, but on his second time around, he mashed the pedal to the floor. He couldn't believe how long the straightaway was. It seemed to stretch out forever in front of him. The banking in the turns was certainly a lot steeper than they looked from the pits, too. Cale tried to remember all the tips he had heard from other drivers and kept his car low going into the turns, letting it drift higher on the turn's exit. He found that he could hold the same line lap after lap and was feeling good about his progress. He was a Grand National driver at the Darlington International Speedway. September 2, 1957, was a red-letter day in Cale's life, that's for sure.

As Cale brought the car into the pits, Johnny Bruner, a NASCAR official, came running over, saying, "You've gotta get out of that car. You're too young." Cale had been caught. He removed his helmet, threw it to Bobby and stomped off, wondering if his dream was shattered before the race even started.

He couldn't believe how long the straightaway was. It seemed to stretch out forever in front of him.

Bobby caught up to him and asked, "Hey, Cale, do you think you got enough laps in to qualify the car?" "I don't know," was the reply. "Besides, how can we do that? I've already been caught." Bobby explained that he had a plan, and as Cale heard it, his excitement returned. It just might work. Bobby steered the car back onto the track and lined up in his qualifying position. He watched the officials intently since now they were keeping a pretty close eye on the #30 car. At just the right moment, he quickly climbed from the car and disappeared into the pits. Cale had been hiding in the passenger floorboard and found his way into the driver's seat.

He was finally waved onto the racing surface for his two quick laps, and he gave it all he had. It felt good as he followed the line he had practiced before, and Cale finished his qualifying run confident that he had been fast. But, as the times were posted, he found that he had qualified 44th out of 53 cars. His time, which had seemed so fast, was a full 10 mph below the top qualifier, Paul Goldsmith. For the first time, he began to feel the doubt. Should he really be here racing against these guys? Did he possess the skills necessary to pilot the car around this track without being in the way? It would be a long race, and he resolved that he would learn from each lap and catch up to the pace quickly.

He climbed from the car, and as he and Bobby were beginning to discuss the qualifying run, they noticed Johnny Bruner coming their way, this time with Norris Friel, another official. They grabbed Cale by the arm, and said, "Let's go." Cale asked, "Where are you taking me?" "Outside the track. That seems to be the only way to keep you out of that car," Norris replied as they walked him outside the gates. Undaunted, Cale knew exactly what to do. He ran to the same spot where he had climbed under the fence when he was 11 years old. He maneuvered under it one more time and was back in the pits before the officials had returned. He blended in with the crowd and found his way back to their pit.

"Gimme that helmet, quick," he told Bobby.

But Bobby didn't want to. "I can't do that Cale," he said. "You've already been caught twice. I'll start the race, and as soon as we can, we'll switch. After the race starts, there will be too much action for them to focus attention on us."

Cale knew he was right. So he just found a place amidst the onlookers, trying to be patient as he waited for just the right time. The drivers all pulled on their helmets, climbed in the cars, and cinched their belts tight. The command, "Gentlemen, start your engines," was followed by the sound of 53 race engines coming to life, accompanied by the roar of the tens of thousands who had gathered to watch. It was enough to raise the hairs on Cale's arms. The cars slowly pulled onto the track for the pace laps. One car stalled, drawing the attention of all the officials, as they went to help. Cale hoped that Bobby had noticed, and he had. After the first pace lap, the #30 car swung into the pits, and the driver change happened so fast that, this time, nobody noticed. Cale moved out onto the track and into position for the start. He intently watched the starter, wanting to get as good a start as possible without drawing attention to himself for jumping out too early. The race was on!

Cale immediately passed a couple of slower cars, but several of the cars from behind went by like a shot. Did he really belong here? The doubt once again crept into his thoughts. He could see the leaders ahead pulling away from the field, but he seemed able to keep up with those in the pack. By Lap 15, Curtis Turner had taken the lead. He had also already lapped Cale's #30 Pontiac. Cale could keep up with the cars he had qualified near, but he had nothing for the fast boys. This was the big league, and maybe he wasn't quite ready. He was sure that, with experience, he could learn to handle a car as well as they could, but for now his best just wasn't good enough. Fonty Flock spun out, hitting the wall, on Lap 18, bringing out the first caution flag. On the restart, once again, the same cars as before pulled away from the field, their lead growing with each lap. There was a hard crash on Lap 27 between Paul Goldsmith and Bobby Myers. Myers was slumped over his steering wheel, and Cale made a conscious effort not to look at him as he made the next few laps. As he rounded Turn 4 on the next lap, he looked up and saw Johnny Bruner, once again, giving him the black flag, meaning that he would have to pull into the pits on the next time around. Caught again. This time he knew that his day was over, so he just pulled the car on into the pits and climbed out. Bobby climbed in and returned to the track. Four laps later, Bobby hit the wall, ending the day for the #30 Pontiac. One of their junkyard spindles had broken. Cale and Bobby became spectators for the rest of the race. Speedy Thompson and Curtis Turner had the fastest cars that day, with Speedy leading the last 150 laps in his 1957 Chevy to take the win.

What a day it had been. It took a couple of hours to repair the car enough to tow it home, and they rode home in a solemn, silent mood. Even though he had been successful in getting to race underage, Cale contemplated how much he had to learn before he could compete with the NASCAR boys. He might be quite a hotshot at the local short tracks, but these guys could drive. Also, he thought about how he had let so many people down. This was a new experience for Cale, and he wasn't quite sure how to respond. *Maybe this racing thing really isn't for me,* he thought as they made their way back to the farm.

The disappointment of the Darlington experience cooled Cale's enthusiasm for racing, and when an offer came from the Sumter Generals to play fullback, he accepted. The Generals, a semipro team, might present an opportunity for him to make up for what he felt was his letting down his benefactors. His success on the field had cemented their support before, and now maybe the same could happen again. There was a common thread between semipro football and racing, though neither paid enough to support him. He would most certainly have to get another job. As he contemplated his next move, he found an old truck in the woods that had been discarded by its owner. Even though the old beast was pretty well used up, Cale saw something in it that moved him. He certainly could bring it back to a working existence, and it raised the idea that he could use it to start a pulpwood business. This way he could be his own boss. He knew it involved hard labor, but maybe the work would help keep him in shape for football. So he went out, bought a two-man crosscut saw and an axe, and the Cale Yarborough Logging Company was in business. He hired a couple men and used a mule to pull the logs from the woods to the truck. Not exactly the best-equipped logging company around, but hard work and a steady supply of trees to cut meant that, within just a small while, he was making about $100 a week. Soon he bought chainsaws, another truck, and a tractor to haul the logs. He was beginning to do pretty well now, and stayed busy between running the company and playing football. But he felt a void, a need for adventure. There had always been some sort of adventure in his life, and he found that without it, he was pretty bored.

Maybe this racing thing really isn't for me, **he thought as they made their way back to the farm.**

Remembering the times with his dad when he was younger, he decided to learn to fly. Why not? Bobby was a pilot. He had learned from a local crop duster who traded lessons for the use of Bobby's motorcycle. So Cale showed up at Bobby's one day with a copy of a *Trade-A-Plane* magazine and said, "Hey, Bobby, let's buy an airplane."

A startled Bobby quipped, "Are you crazy? What happened, did you find gold out there in the woods or what?"

"No," Cale replied, "but there's a J4 Piper Cub in here for $600 up in Ohio."

Bobby took one look at the ad and joined Cale's excitement, saying, "Meet me at Vince McDaniel's store tonight, and we'll talk about it."

That evening they planned to go to Ohio to look at the plane. A friend, Pete Workman, was invited to join in. They were also able to convince Olin Spears to go. Olin was quite an experienced pilot, and, if the plane would fly, maybe he could help them to get it back. This was Cale's first road trip out of the Carolinas, and the winding mountain roads of West Virginia made him carsick—really carsick, in fact— bad enough to make a nuisance of himself in the car. They were all thankful to finally reach Ohio.

The plane wasn't the prettiest thing to look at, but Olin deemed it mechanically sound and capable of flight, so a deal was struck at $575. Now the boys owned an airplane. Cale immediately decided to fly back with Olin to avoid another mountain ride. Flying toward the Carolinas, they encountered bad weather and had to land in Asheville. They waited out the storm, so Bobby and Pete beat them home. The foul weather continued for a few days, so all the boys could do was sit around and talk about flying. Bobby's brother Wib joined in, bragging about his great piloting skills. Not to be outdone, Cale began his boast, that he was probably the greatest pilot ever born. Anyway, the conversation ended with a contest to see who could fly the plane the best. They went out to the field where the Cub was parked. "You can have the left seat," Cale told Wib as they climbed aboard the old craft. "No, it's your plane, so I'll take the co-pilot's seat," Wib shot back. Neither boy had much of an idea how to really fly the plane, but neither would abandon his ruse, thinking the other could bail him out if he got into real trouble. Cale got the plane started, taxied out into the field, and actually took off, using what little he had learned watching his dad and Olin fly

So he went out, bought a two-man crosscut saw and an axe, and the Cale Yarborough Logging Company was in business.

before. This isn't too hard, he thought as he and Wib began to enjoy their flight. Cale experimented with turns, climbs, and generally began to get the feel for the old Cub. All the while, Wib just figured Cale was showing off his skills. Cale asked several times, "Wib, you want to take over?" And each time Wib would return, "No, Cale, you're doing fine." They had been up for about an hour when both daylight and fuel began to run low. Cale had no problem finding his way back. He just followed the highway, knowing that landing the plane was going to present quite a problem.

"Wib, I'd like you to land the plane. You haven't flown it yet, and I'd like you to get the feel of it," Cale urged.

Wib declined.

Cale insisted several times until Wib confessed, "Cale, I've got something I need to tell you. I've never flown a plane before."

Cale sheepishly looked at Wib, "I haven't either."

Realization can slap you in the face. "Oh well, we are just going to have to land it," Cale resolved. His mind considered that landing must be the opposite of taking off, so he would just reverse the procedure. They circled the field, and Cale began to bring the plane in. All was well, but he couldn't get the plane to meet the ground. He would get really low, then he would feel the plane cushion upward, as if there was an invisible force preventing him from landing. After several attempts, their fuel was just about spent. They figured they had one more attempt before they would be completely empty. Cale flew downward toward the field, and at what he felt was the appropriate moment, he shut off the engine. The plane fell the last few feet to the ground, bounced twice, then settled into a skidding halt. "That wasn't so bad, was it, Wib?" Wib couldn't answer. He just headed for his car and left straight away.

The rough landing had its affect on the spindly landing gear, and the right side was now several inches shorter than the left. They nicknamed the plane

"Chester" after the limping deputy on the *Gunsmoke* television show. Cale was able to salvage some pieces from an old plane and piecemeal repair the gear. Then he proceeded to fly all day until he learned to control the plane like a pro. He, Bobby, and Pete flew the plane daily. Pete had an incident with a strong wind gust that flipped the plane upside down and, in turn, sold his share of the plane back to the others for $200. Bobby and Cale repaired the damage and continued to learn and enjoy the old plane. Of course, it didn't take long before they were both bored with it. An old Piper Cub doesn't offer much in the way of power or range, and they both were beginning to want more. They asked Olin to come over and fly the plane, so they could get out on the wings in flight, like they had seen in the movies. The Cub could not achieve enough speed for takeoff, though, so that idea wasn't going to work.

The desire for danger could not be filled by the old Piper Cub, but their determination soon led to a solution. Cale had installed a Continental tire kit to the rear of his convertible, and, looking at it, Cale had an idea. He looked at Bobby and said, "I'll bet you a hamburger at the drive-in that you can't ride the rear bumper of my convertible up and down the runway without being thrown off." Never one to back down from such a bet, Bobby accepted the challenge, and down the runway they went, with Bobby holding on for dear life. Cale gave him quite a ride, all the while increasing the difficulty, beginning to swerve right to left in an outright effort to throw Bobby from the car. He charged toward the edge of the runway as if he would head across the adjacent field. At the last second, he swung the Ford hard left, back toward the runway. The sudden move caught Bobby unaware, and he flew from the bumper into the kudzu aligning the edge of the field. Thankfully, the kudzu was thick, breaking his fall and preventing injury.

Neither boy had much of an idea how to really fly the plane, but neither would abandon his ruse, thinking the other could bail him out if he got into real trouble.

Cale laughed at the result and called out to Bobby, "I told you so. I knew you couldn't hang on forever. You owe me a hamburger."

"Not so fast, Cale," Bobby said. "You've got to give me a chance to win it back. Jump up on the rear bumper of my pickup. I'll sling you out into the field."

"You'll do no such thing," Cale replied. "I can hang on no matter if you flip that truck. You won't get me back that easy."

Bobby climbed into the cab of the new truck. Cale climbed upon the rear bumper, getting a good hold on the rubber-coated chains that held the tailgate shut. It reminded Cale of water skiing. Bobby took off across the field, swerving side to side, faster and faster. Still, Cale was holding on. Bobby increased his efforts to no avail until he tried to turn just a little too hard at speed. The dirt built up under the tires as they slid sideways and, sure enough, the truck rolled over. The momentum of the roll carried the pickup a complete revolution, and the truck landed back on its wheels. Cale found time to release his grip on the truck, and, this time, he was the one flying through the air into the kudzu. He landed on his shoulder, and although the immediate pain was rather intense, he got up, wiped the dust from his pants and made sure everything was intact. The same could not be said of the truck—its roof was flattened, the front and rear windows now gone. But it could still be driven. "Well, I guess you don't have to buy me a hamburger," Cale reminded Bobby as they both broke out in hysterical laughter.

It seemed to Cale that maybe stunts in the air would be a little safer than being thrown from the rear of a high-speed land vehicle. Aeronautics seemed the next logical step. Cale spent a few days planning. A loop, he figured, would be the best stunt with which to begin. A loop should be easy enough—just pull back on the stick as the plane reached the apex of the loop, then push the stick forward to complete the maneuver. His first try started well enough until he was upside down, but then the plane stalled. He had not entered the roll with enough speed. Cale had somewhat already planned for such, and righted the plane.

His next few attempts began to go smoother until, on about the fifth try, he looped it right over. A little more practice, and the stunt was mastered. It was time to move on.

Harold Lyles hung around the airfield quite a bit. He was a skydiver, but he didn't have his own plane. Cale and Bobby worked out a deal with him to take him up for some jumps if he would teach them how to jump and let them use his parachute. Since the old Cub would only seat two, they had to take turns flying with Harold to learn their lessons. He had them watch a few jumps as he explained how and when to deploy the chute, how to guide it through the air, and how to land and roll. On one last jump with Bobby, he announced that they could have the chute. "And if it doesn't work," he told them, "I'll give you another one."

Cale, of course, jumped right up and said, "Let me go first." Bobby was happy to let Cale go first, and replied, "Be my guest." With Harold's direction, Cale strapped on the chute pack and struggled to make his way into the cockpit. Bobby climbed into the pilot's seat, and they soon were cruising over the field at 3,000 feet. Cale climbed out onto the wing strut, yelled, "Geronimo!" and released himself from the plane. What a feeling! The air rushed by with little sound, the plane was speeding off into the distance, and he was falling toward the ground at a much faster pace than he had imagined. He pulled the ripcord, and the chute released itself from its packing, gathered in the air, and halted his downward plunge with enough force to make him feel as if he were actually going upward. Gathering his thoughts, Cale began to plan his landing. He carefully remembered all that Harold had told him, but as he looked down, he realized that he was still falling at a pretty quick pace. Also, he seemed to be drifting toward the woods, and fought the chute ropes to steer clear of any trouble. The ground came up quickly, and Cale landed on the edge of the field feet first. The force of the landing made him feel as if his legs were driven up into his chest, and the pain stunned him for a moment. He gathered his faculties and checked that nothing was broken or hurt badly, gathered up the chute, and began running across the field to where Bobby had landed the plane, yelling, "Bobby, Bobby, you've gotta try this. This might be the best thing since sliced bread." The exhilaration of the jump far outweighed any pain associated with the landing, and he wanted his friend to share the feeling.

They discussed the jump for a minute, with Cale's enthusiasm dominating the conversation. It was as if he knew all there was to know about parachuting. They stuffed the chute back into the pack, and Cale helped Bobby strap in. This time, Cale jumped into the pilot's seat, and soon the plane was climbing back into the sky. As they flew across the field, Bobby stepped out and jumped. Cale circled and landed, watching Bobby as he floated toward him. Shortly, Bobby landed, and Cale ran to see how Bobby had fared. What he found stopped him in his tracks. The chute straps had not been properly attached under Bobby's legs, and when the chute had deployed, they had immediately risen to beneath his arms. He had clutched the ropes so tightly all the way down that his hands were numb with pain, and his face was flush with color. "Cale, you've got a lot to learn about parachuting," he snorted. After a brief respite to catch their breath, they spent the rest of the day taking turns jumping, one after the other, until they were getting to be pretty good at it. The next day, they went to the Army-Navy store and bought a surplus chute. It became their passion for the next few weeks, jumping almost every day.

Cale climbed out onto the wing strut, yelled, "Geronimo!" and released himself from the plane.

The wear and tear on the old airplane was beginning to take its toll, and repairs were becoming more frequent. The logging business had been a little slow, so the plane budget dwindled. One day as they were jumping, Cale had an idea. He had noticed that many times there would be cars parked alongside the roads, and the passengers would emerge to watch them as they guided the chute to earth. "Bobby," he told his friend, "I bet we could put on an air show and get people to pay to watch us." They bounced the idea back and forth and formed a plan to include a ground show where the people could gather and they could collect. As the plan developed, they included Bobby's brothers Irby and Wib, and let Harold in on it as well. They bought a couple old cars and built some ramps where Cale could perform some rolls and jumps from ramp to ramp. They found a field near a busy highway over in Cartersville that was perfect.

The first couple weeks, they didn't draw much attention, but soon word spread of the "thrill show," and the crowd grew. An old PA system was found, with Irby on the microphone sounding just like a professional announcer: "Ladies and gentlemen, here he is, that famous race car driver direct from the Southern 500 at Darlington, Cale Yarborough. God go with you, Cale." Cale would pull the old car onto the field, spin around a little, then hit the ramps for a few rolls and jumps. Then Harold would fly them up one at a time for the parachute jumps. To finish the show, Cale would take the plane up for an aerobatic exhibition of rolls, loops, and stalls. It was working, as cars began lining the streets. The next week, they hired a country western band out of Florence led by Slim Mims, who went by the name of Uncle Ugly. He would dress in a crazy country outfit and perform a comedy routine as a part of the entertainment.

They had flyers made and advertised the upcoming week's show. Cale was worried that he would be upstaged by Uncle Ugly, so he decided to bring the race car out of mothballs for a special jump. They made a new set of ramps, bigger and higher than the last. They called the race car jump the "Jump from Hell" and would perform it as the show's finale after the aerobatics. Between the flyers and word of mouth, quite a crowd assembled to watch the show, enough, in fact, to warrant state troopers directing traffic. "Folks, we ask $1 per car contribution to keep the show going. One of our people will be by to collect," Irby announced as Wib went car to car for the money. Cale did his preliminary rolls and jumps with the old cars, and Uncle Ugly played while the plane made trek after trek into the skies above for the jumps and tricks. Then Cale strapped on his helmet and climbed into the old race car. He had not sat in the car for several months now, and it felt good to be back behind the wheel. The roar of the big V8 reverberated among the crowd as he pulled the car to the edge of the field. Bobby had tried to get Cale to make a practice jump, but Cale had resisted, so confident he was. He revved the engine, let out the clutch, and sped toward the ramp. The car climbed the ramp and flew into the air. Cale

> **"Ladies and gentlemen, here he is, that famous race car driver direct from the Southern 500 at Darlington, Cale Yarborough. God go with you, Cale."**

watched below as the landing ramp came into sight, then passed beneath as he sailed over. The car cleared the entire ramp and landed hard on its nose before flipping three times, finally stopping on its side. Not exactly as planned, but as Cale climbed from the upturned window, the crowd cheered wildly. It was the best thrill show they had ever seen. The old race car had made its last run, though, and Cale was ready to shelve the whole show. Even with the crowd they had attracted, there was not enough money involved to replace the race car, much less the bumps and bruises, preparation time, and all the effort it had taken to present the show. He sure enjoyed getting back in the race car, though.

Word spread of the thrill show across the state, and a couple of weeks later one of the organizers of the Beaufort Water Festival contacted Cale, making him an offer to perform parachute jumps with Harold for their festival for $50 each. They had not cleared that kind of money on the entire thrill show, so they readily accepted. The two of them drove down to Beaufort and arrived as the parade was in progress.

They were impressed with the setup. Quite a crowd was on hand, as the weather was good, although a little windy. There were street vendors, boat races, bands, banners, and, overall, a carnival-like atmosphere persisted. The organizers had arranged for two Piper Cubs, one for each jumper. Their plan was for the two of them to jump into the bay from 10,000 feet. Cale had never even been that high, and had certainly never jumped from such an altitude. He didn't see a problem, though, figuring that a higher altitude just meant it would take longer to fall to the earth. When it was time, Cale and Harold suited up, strapped on their chutes, and climbed into their crafts.

The two planes took off and sailed into the skies above the festival. It was beautiful from above, with all the commotion and colors below them. Cale had also never jumped into water, but landing in the drink had to be softer than landing on the ground, didn't it? The two Cubs struggled to reach 8,000 feet in the wind conditions, and it became obvious that this was going to be their maximum height. Cale watched Harold climb onto the strut and release from the plane. He followed, and the two of them were above the bay, falling to earth in a free fall that lasted twice as long as Cale was accustomed. The chutes opened simultaneously as the crowd below craned their necks and pointed at the skydivers. As they began their drifting descent, Cale noticed that he and Harold were getting farther and farther from each other. Harold was headed for the bay, but Cale found that he was moving over the town, away from the water. He fought the ropes to regain position over the water, but continued to float inland. He knew he would miss the target, so he began to search the landscape for a suitable place to land. The closer he came to the landing, the taller the trees, buildings, and power lines loomed. The fact was that he was going to land where he was going to land, and planning would have nothing to do with it. He was headed straight for a power line, and saw that he would be hard-pressed to miss it. As he approached, he pulled his legs up and over the wires, just clearing them. The move saved him from the lines but deposited him on the roof of a dentist's building. The local fire department came to the rescue, bringing a ladder and plucking him from the roof. Cale was unhurt, except for his pride. He had come all the way down to Beaufort to put on a show and ended up having to be rescued from the top of a building, having missed the bay completely. How embarrassing!

The next week, Cale and Bobby were out in their old Cub, jumping again, and Cale was sitting at the edge of the plane getting ready to jump. Suddenly the turbulence from a thermal blast rocked the little plane, and threw him into the sky before he had completely strapped into his chute. The unexpected free fall found him trying with all his faculties to get the rest of his chute fastened, but he was unsuccessful. His fear was that when the chute opened, the force would take it completely from him. He struggled to find the ripcord, held onto the chute with all his might, and anticipated the sudden stop when the chute opened. The chute disengaged from the pack, but refused to open properly, with only part of it catching the wind and slowing his downward progress. Cale knew that he was falling too fast, but there was little he could do about it. He readied himself for the hardest landing of his life, and fell in a heap in the midst of a freshly plowed field. Oh, how he hurt. He felt sure that he was all broken up, but found everything was still in some sort of order. The soft dirt and partial chute opening had been just enough to prevent serious injury. He had fallen from an airplane and survived. Maybe someone was trying to send him a message. He decided at that moment that his jumping days were over, and that he would get back into racing. He traded his share in the old Piper to Bobby for a couple of chainsaws and an old farm wagon. It was time to go looking for another good ride.

Maybe someone was trying to send him a message. He decided at that moment that his jumping days were over, and that he would get back into racing.

No good rides became available for a while, so he and Bobby bought an old boat and learned to water ski at their old water hole on the Lynches. There wasn't really enough room to ski there, so they cut a few of the cypresses to make way. They now had more room, but it was like skiing an obstacle course, as all the stumps were at the water line. Again, traffic would stop and watch them as they sped around the course. Cale certainly loved the attention, and again felt like a showman. He also decided to join the rodeo in Florence. He had ridden bulls on the farm before, so it just seemed a natural fit. The only problem was that, in learning the skill of riding, there is a lot of being thrown off. It's the same for everybody, so Cale just looked at it as being part of the business. He quickly tired of becoming more friendly with the ground than the bull, though. It reminded him of a saying his dad had taught him, a saying that he had adopted as his motto: "There's never a horse that couldn't be rode...and there's never a cowboy that couldn't be throwed." The horses and bulls in the rodeo certainly made a believer of him, and he decided that this would be his last attempt at show business.

CHAPTER 4

The Racer

Persistence pays. The old saying certainly had meaning in Cale's life. He had become a fixture at the local racetracks. There was a track of some sort in almost every town. Most were the same, just a field where a grader had fashioned an oval of some proportion. Constant erosion of the surfaces demanded steady maintenance just to keep them drivable. So every time you would race at a particular track, it would be a little different than last time, just depending on how good the driver of the grader was at his task. All the tracks had wooden bleachers up and down one side of the track. There were also wooden fences and guardrails defining the edges of the racing surface. Fans would watch from the bleachers or at a favorite site around the fence as they devoured hot dogs and popcorn, drank soft drinks, and smoked or chewed tobacco. There were always plenty of fans, no matter the track.

You could always find Cale in the infield, walking from pit to pit, looking for a team that might need a driver. He had a knack for it, and most times he would end up in a car, even if it was not the best car. Sometimes he found himself behind the wheel of an old rust bucket that had no business on the track. And sometimes he would end up with a fairly competitive ride. He would never know until just before race time whether he would be able to race or not, so he certainly couldn't anticipate which car he might be strapped into. It didn't matter what kind of car he was in, though. He would always give it all he had, many times making a bad car look pretty good. His aggressive style began to draw some attention, and the other drivers began to respect him. This made it easier to find quality rides, and as the weeks rolled by, the cars he piloted became better and better. With the improved equipment, he became more and more competitive, finishing at or near the front of the pack more often.

You could always find Cale in the infield, walking from pit to pit, looking for a team that might need a driver.

Columbia was Cale's favorite place to race for several reasons. First, it wasn't too far away, so it didn't cost much to get there. Racing, up to this point, offered very little money for a racer like Cale, so gas money to and from the track was always a consideration. Besides, he was usually unsure as to whether or not he would even be racing, so he had to be prepared.

Another reason he liked Columbia so much was the track itself. Most racetracks in the South consisted of a mixture of red clay and sand, making for a tractable surface that usually stayed fairly stable, with grooves rutting out as the evening progressed. The track in Columbia and most of those tracks throughout central South Carolina were cut from fields of white clay called "bull tallow." Bull tallow has a completely different consistency than its red cousin. Whereas the red clay bonds somewhat to itself, the wear patterns tend to be generally uniform. The white tallow won't stick to anything and, as it wears, large chunks of it will come out at once, leaving holes sometimes almost as large as the cars that are trying to race around them. These holes normally form through the turns as the multiple forces of the tires eat the surface lap by lap. These white clay tracks were the ones Cale had cut his racing teeth on, so he was quite accustomed to handling a car on such a surface. Columbia's surface attracted some of the best drivers of the period, and this was the real reason Cale liked this track so much. David Pearson, Bobby Isaac, Lee Roy Yarbrough, Tiny Lund, Tom Pistone, Ralph Earnhardt, Curtis Turner, and other NASCAR stars would show up on any given Thursday night to challenge the track. Typically they would line up against the locals and other drivers from the "swamp" areas of the region, drivers like Rock Raines and J.D. "Junior" Johnson.

It really was no wonder that the pros would show up at Columbia. These guys were real racers, men who could stare down any challenge. And what a challenge a Thursday night at Columbia could be. The track presented its own obstacles, but the field of drivers was always a mix of pros and newcomers. This was one track where Cale could line up against the best and give it a go. The first rides he was offered weren't exactly up to par, but neither was Cale. It was quite obvious that to some of the pros who would enter the Thursday night events, racing was a different sport than the one Cale had been used to at the local outlaw tracks. These drivers could charge as hard as anyone, but they were also cunning in their moves, timing their passes to the least dangerous moments. Cale paid attention to their actions and took every opportunity to talk to them in the pits, hoping to pick up tips. Many times the rides he was able to climb into would break, leading to an early departure from the contest. Still, Cale would try to wring all he could from each and every chance he was given. When the cars would break, it was usually no fault of his. The car owners generally understood this, leaving an opportunity to drive for them at another time.

Racing was becoming the focal point of Cale's life. Bobby had bought a car to campaign on the outlaw tracks, and Cale would always be there in the pits, helping to crew the car. That is, unless he could scrounge a ride from one of the other owners. The experience of driving a different car each week was becoming commonplace for Cale. As a result, he became adept at assessing a car's abilities very quickly. He didn't have a choice if he was going to place anywhere in the money. Placing in the money was becoming more important, as his trips to and from the track were becoming somewhat of a financial burden. Even when they would have a good race, it often paid for little more than their gas. Any money Cale would win would have to be split with whoever owned the car he had driven that particular night. Weekly exposure was helping Cale to build on his young reputation, though, and his skills and track savvy were growing with each time out. Sometimes tracks would offer appearance money to the favorite drivers in addition to any money they might win. Cale would often call ahead of the race to see if any of that money would be available to him. Even though the answer would most often be "No," occasionally there would be $5 or $10 to help pay expenses and gas. He was beginning to work his way into the better rides, and his finishes began to reflect the difference.

Cale was gaining a reputation by pushing these rides to better finishes than expected, and more owners were open to putting him behind the wheel of their rides. It seemed that he was more often finding himself toward the front of the pack at the end of the night's activities. He was also gaining confidence in his style and his abilities to read the track, the traffic, and the mishaps. It was an ideal place to learn. A typical night at the track could involve mechanical havoc. Tempers would often flare, and a stock car can be a mighty powerful weapon. It wasn't uncommon to be rammed in the door by the guy you passed with two laps to go, or to be hit in the rear by the driver you tried to run off the track. And when they would come out of the relative safety of the cockpit, rivals would quickly resort to fisticuffs. Cale learned early that these seasoned warriors would never develop respect for him unless he stood up to them. His hard-charging style evoked the ire of others, so his race car often came home with several dents not caused by racing accidents, and there were many nights when he would climb out of the driver's side window with his mouth and his fists in full motion. It didn't take too long before he was no longer considered a rookie. He was invited into the fraternity that he'd always dreamed of, and it was all happening pretty quickly.

Weekly exposure was helping Cale to build on his young reputation, though, and his skills and track savvy were growing with each time out.

One night in Columbia, Cale got a big break. Curtis Crider climbed from his car, succumbing to the pressure on the track. It was a particularly raucous event, with all the drivers beating and banging on each other. Curtis had a good race car, and Cale knew it, so he had his helmet on before Curtis could even climb from the machine. Cale jumped in and gunned it for the track. He was really moving by the time he came around to the first turn. There had formed in the middle of the turn a hole just about big enough to park a Volkswagen in. Cale didn't know about it and hit it square on. The force threw the car into the air, through the rail, and over the outer fence. He ended up driving through the parking lot, swerving around to miss the parked cars as he slowed the car to a stop. As he returned to the pits, Curtis said, "Oh yeah, I meant to tell you, there's a big hole going into Turn 1." They all had a good laugh, but Cale felt as if he had missed a good chance to show just what he could do behind the wheel. It had definitely been the best piece he had ever driven against these guys, and he knew he would have had a fighting chance if he had not crashed out.

Cale had caught the attention of a car builder named Marion "the Preacher" Cox, who ran two 1937 Fords with the powerful overhead valve V8s. Jimmy Thompson, Speedy's brother, was his primary driver, but he needed a driver to pilot his second car at the half-mile asphalt track at Myrtle Beach. Marion tapped Cale for the ride. The Cox cars were known to be good cars, and Cale saw this as his first big break. Also, it was a chance to see what he could do on asphalt. The Myrtle Beach track had started as a dirt oval, but the addition of the asphalt had added a new dimension to the racing. Speeds climbed, reflecting the better traction, and, for the first time, Cale was driving around a short track where he could see clearly. One of the constants at all the dirt tracks was the dust. All the commotion caused by 20 to 30 race cars churning a short dirt track would create an atmosphere that made it very difficult to see. Sometimes a driver would follow so closely that, when an opponent would make a mistake, the driver would follow suit. There were times when Cale would follow a car into the pits without realizing it or find himself against an outside wall he had not yet seen. The asphalt would present his next racing challenge.

Cale began to prove himself on the paved track and became the number two driver for the Cox team. Only several races later, on a beautiful starlit night, Cale took the checkered flag in the featured event. He had bested them all, including Jimmy Thompson. The next week yielded the same result, and Jimmy began to complain to Marion that Cale might be the number two driver, but he was getting the number one equipment. Marion could see the logic and agreed to let the two switch cars for the next race. Again, this time in Jimmy's car, Cale won the race. Never again would Jimmy complain about equipment to Marion. Cale's confidence was sparked by the good race car and fueled by the wins. He was beginning to like the asphalt and the speeds possible on it. Just about the time he was beginning to feel comfortable, they tore up the asphalt and reverted back to dirt. The speeds generated on asphalt quickly wore out tires, making it more expensive to race there. Some car owners were staying away because of this, and the field had grown smaller. The switch back to dirt made no difference. Cale continued winning, a combination of a good car and newfound confidence. The asphalt had added a new dimension with the increased speeds. Cale began to see himself as a more capable driver and yearned for another try against the pros. He decided to give Darlington

Cale took the checkered flag in the featured event. He had bested them all, including Jimmy Thompson.

another try. He had gained several years' experience and felt he was ready. Bobby Lee, of Sumter, had a Ford that he campaigned. He offered the ride to Cale, thinking Cale had a better chance than he at the speedway. Cale was still a year younger than the rules allowed, but he knew that he could fake it. He was no longer looked at as a rookie and had raced against these guys so often on the dirt tracks that they trusted him to not make stupid mistakes. He sent in his paperwork and again was afforded the proper credentials to run at Darlington for the 1959 Southern 500.

Joe Weatherly was staying at the Darlington Motel, and Cale stopped by one night before a race. He was welcomed in and joined the festivities. There were a couple of girls there, and Joe was talking about flying. He offered to take the girls up for a midnight flight and asked Cale to join them. Cale knew that most of the drivers could fly, but he also knew that they knew little about instruments and such, and he was more than a little leery about accepting the offer. Joe winked at him a couple of times as a signal, and finally Cale and the girls agreed on a trip to the airfield for a quick flight. It was pitch dark at the field as Joe approached his plane, which was tethered beside the strip. The three passengers climbed aboard as Joe went around the plane for his preflight routine. Cale noticed that he had not released the tether lines, but when Joe boarded he winked at Cale again, so nothing was said. Joe started the engine, moved the stick forward as if to move forward. The plane strained at the lines, but did not move, other than the vibration caused by the engine's thwarted efforts. "Hold on, now, here we go," Joe said and readied his guests as he acted out the whole scene. He was working the controls feverishly, putting on quite a show. The girls were impressed and let it be known that they had never flown before. Joe led them through the ride, explaining that they were now airborne and pretending to fly them through the night sky. After a few minutes, he prepared them for what was supposed to be a landing. The girls held on tight as he pushed the stick forward in a motion that would bring the plane back to earth. Playing the throttle just right, he simulated a perfect landing and taxi, and then shut the engine down.

"So, how was it, girls?" he asked as the plane's engine shuddered to a stop.

"Wow, that was great, and nothing like we thought it would be," they chimed.

They all climbed from the craft, got in Cale's convertible, and drove back to the motel. What a flight it had been, and the plane had never left the ground.

The next day was race day, and enthusiasm was high as the day began bright and hot. With Bobby Lee's car, Cale had daydreams of running up front and maybe lapping the field. Sometimes dreams are just dreams, and the race itself turned out to be quite anticlimactic. From the green flag, Cale had been able to run midpack, passing and being passed. The car settled into a groove, and the track that was "too tough to tame" was beginning to feel more and more familiar. Not comfortable, just more familiar, mind you. Cale was relegated to his midpack position until the engine internals broke, sending oil and smoke across the track, ending his day.

Stepping back into the big leagues, as he had done in Darlington, reminded Cale again that he was a small fish in a large pond. He knew that he was not quite ready for the leap to NASCAR, so he went back to driving Marion Cox's car at the better short tracks, with some success. He was proud to be a part of Cox's team. Marion's budget wasn't the largest, but he had his own garage and he put together good race cars. Several of the best sportsman and modified drivers had fielded Marion's cars, including Speedy and Jimmy Thompson. Driving for Marion meant that he had a steady ride and was able to show up and run most of the larger venues in the area competitively. He began forming relationships with the other drivers and really becoming part of the racing family. Racing relationships often seem contradictory. As competitors, the guys beat and bang their cars together on the track. They take advantage of every possible opportunity, set off each other's tempers, and even fight over track situations. After the race, however, you are likely to see a group of drivers out together for hamburgers and a few laughs. Their bond was a fiercely competitive spirit, individually contained but collectively expressed. Each was convinced of his own excellence, and each was willing to protect and defend that belief.

Stepping back into the big leagues, as he had done in Darlington, reminded Cale again that he was a small fish in a large pond.

Bobby Atkinson joined Bobby Weatherly and Cale at the track and became part of the crew. The three pooled their resources and bought an old '37 Plymouth with a 276-cubic-inch DeSoto Firedome engine to run at the outlaw tracks. It was the hottest car Cale had ever been able to field in these events, and he won his share of races. Between running his own car and driving the Cox machine, racing was beginning to occupy more of his time, effort, and thought. Success on the dirt tracks came more frequently, meaning that paydays came more regularly and became more substantial.

One night, after a win in Columbia in Marion's car, Cale found himself with $300 in his pocket. Sometimes the drivers would stop by a place called The Hitchin' Post for a hot dog and a beer. Tonight would be different—Cale would spring for their best steak for everybody. Everybody included Bobby, Cale, and all the guys who helped at Marion's shop with the car. There were a total of 12, and they all placed their orders. Time passed, and the food had yet to be served. About an hour later, a wedding party walked through the door, the girls in their long, beautiful dresses and the guys in their freshly pressed tuxes. It was quite a contrast to the group of racers, covered with dirt and grease from the night's competition. The wedding party took their seats and placed their orders. The racers were still waiting for their food. Several minutes later, the racers noticed that the wedding party was being served and that they were all having steaks.

Cale strolled over to their table and exclaimed to the head of the table, "Hey, I believe those are our steaks."

The man replied, "I don't believe they are. You must be in the wrong place, boy."

Cale considered that the wrong answer, reached down, grabbed the steak, and took a big bite of it. "It tastes like my steak to me," he said.

The man stood up from the table, and before he could get fully to his feet, Cale hit him square in the jaw, knocking him against the table. Steak, bread, and iced tea all hit the floor, as the table's occupants all jumped up to avoid the mess. Suddenly the whole place erupted into a scene from a Wild West movie. Everybody in the place began fighting, even the women. Fists and chairs were flying. Certain that the police would soon be there, Cale informed each of his crew members to leave the building. As Cale himself was looking for the door, he was hit from behind with a chair and knocked to the ground. He crawled through the door and rose to dust himself off. Just then, the police arrived. "You'd better hurry up and get in there," Cale told the lawman. "There's the awfullest fight I ever saw." The policemen hurried through the door to stop the madness. Cale and his crew jumped into their trucks and headed for home. They had stopped for their last time at The Hitchin' Post.

Cale considered that the wrong answer, reached down, grabbed the steak, and took a big bite of it. "It tastes like my steak to me," he said.

Cale still found some time to go to the closest NASCAR events, combing the pits and looking for an opportunity to drive. He still held his NASCAR license, so why not? Occasionally, he would find a ride for the day, but most often the equipment was not up to the task and Cale's day would be cut short by failing parts. In 1960, he and Bobby Weatherly went to Daytona for the second Daytona 500. The inaugural run ended with Lee Petty beating Johnny Beauchamp in a very close race. Bobby and Cale went down to see just what a two-and-a-half mile racetrack looked like. They arrived at the track during an early practice, and, as luck would have it, Cale found himself in the right place at the right time. One of the car owners, Roger Odom from Charleston, South Carolina, had brought a '55 Chevy that had been converted from a drag car. The combination of the car and the track proved more than Roger could handle, and he asked Cale to drive for him. He had seen Cale run on a short track, and knew Cale's abilities were above his own. Cale was in the car immediately, with almost the entire practice session to become familiar with his situation. His first lap at Daytona was unbelievable. The Darlington track had offered one-and-a-half miles of racing surface, and it seemed as if the extra mile at Daytona would go on forever. However, by the end of the session, he felt quite at home and was excited about his upcoming qualifying run. Qualifying would take place just before the modified/sportsman race, and there were about 50,000 people in the stands. The run went well, with the old '55 starting the race well up in the pack at over 140 mph. Top speeds were reaching 170 mph, much faster than Cale had run on the short tracks he was accustomed to. He anticipated the green flag almost perfectly and found himself leading the race after only a few laps. It was as if this was the kind of racing Cale had always been meant to run, as, lap after lap, he led the cars around the oval. He settled into the rhythm of the car, feeling more comfortable with each passing lap. The high banks at each end of the speedway began to feel natural, and his race could not have been going better. That is, until, with about 20 laps to go, Cale began to hear a familiar grumbling from beneath the hood of the Chevy. Suddenly, the oil pressure gauge sank to zero, and the cockpit began to fill with the acrid oil smoke that accompanies such a disintegration. He found the apron of the track and managed to get back to the pits without incident. The blown engine reminded Cale of something he had heard Curtis Turner say at the dirt track one night: "If a man runs his car as hard as it will go, it is going to be real hard on the equipment. There's going to be things that break. It's just the way it is."

After Daytona, it was back to South Carolina and his usual life of logging and running the short tracks. Racing was a little different, though, as Cale's confidence level had been elevated by the Daytona experience. He had led in "the big one" for much of the race, putting him among a very elite group. This level of confidence began to show up at the track, with his finishes becoming more and more consistently toward the front. Pole positions and wins were becoming much more a part of his vocabulary.

He had little luck at the NASCAR tracks until the 1963 season, when he hooked up with a car owner/builder named Herman Beam. Herman lived in Johnson City, Tennessee, and was known to build a pretty good car. Up to this point in Cale's NASCAR career, he had only been able to compete in a handful of races over the span of several seasons, and Herman offered an opportunity, if he ran well, to enter the fray on a more consistent basis. They campaigned the Myrtle Beach, Savannah, Bristol, and Greenville short track events together with great success. Cale finished two of the races in the top 10. Herman had tried several drivers early in the season, but now he had found his man. The relationship warmed, and Herman decided he was ready to go after the Grand National circuit in earnest. Their next event, at Nashville, was the start of a partnership that would last until late in the 1964 season. Herman's cars had never run better, as Cale produced seven top 10s and three top fives during the 1963 campaign.

There was a bond between the drivers of the Grand National circuit that was hard to explain. Each driver was exceptional in his own way, but some of the characters were much larger than life. Such was certainly the case for Curtis Turner, who had taken a special liking to Cale. Curtis was the brashest of them all, and a constant party always followed him. All the other drivers wondered how he could climb into his race car, with all the noise and commotion, after late nights of very heavy drinking. However he did it, when he strapped his helmet on, he was ready to take the track with all the ferocity his equipment would allow. His was the car swinging the widest, braking the latest, literally fighting its way toward the front. Even when he didn't win, he put on a show. It was an attitude he carried home with him, as he lived the rest of his life in a similar fashion.

It was as if this was the kind of racing Cale had always been meant to run, as, lap after lap, he led the cars around the oval.

Curtis lived in a big house, with a huge patio out back where he could throw his parties. Cale was over one day, and Curtis began to explain the Darlington track to Cale. In the midst of his explanation, he said, "Here, let me show you." He went out to his shed and pulled up on his patio on his tractor. The tractor went round and round the patio as Curtis explained that Turns 3 and 4 were not as steep in the banking and needed to be negotiated with a totally different approach. His explanation became so animated that he knocked the railing off one side of the patio. It was a lesson Cale would not forget.

In early 1964, Cale's logging business was on the brink of extinction. Although he raced frequently, the money he was bringing home from the track seemed only to pay for the good times he was having after the races. Cale picked up a few part-time jobs to fill the gap, including one milking cows for one of his cousins in Olanta. He had become so busy with racing and work that his social life had taken a plunge. In fact, he hardly had one at all. He began to feel the need for female companionship in his life, something that had been missing for some time. He had heard that there was a cute girl working in Olanta at the drugstore, so one day after milking the cows, he combed his hair, entered the drugstore, and ordered a milk shake. Self-confidence had never been lacking in Cale, but the girl he saw behind the counter was unlike any he had ever seen. She wasn't just cute to him, she was beautiful. He was immediately smitten, and the drugstore became a regular stopping place after work. Soon they were out together, Cale and Betty Jo Thigpen, at the local drive-in and the movie theater. Where they were didn't matter, as long as they were together. She was as taken as Cale was, and the two became inseparable. Betty Jo's parents weren't exactly thrilled. They knew the reputations of the race car drivers, and it did not necessarily fit with their dreams for their daughter. Betty Jo tried to ease them by telling them that Cale was always a perfect gentleman, and that the racers' reputations did not matter.

Now that Cale was in love, his life had acquired a totally new dimension.

Herman had Cale busier than they had been in '63, and they began entering most of the Grand National events. They were consistently finishing in the top 15, with several top 10s thrown in here and there. Again, Cale was finishing almost every race, protecting the equipment to satisfy Herman. He was learning how to manage his natural on-track aggression with good reasoning, and it was paying dividends. He was becoming better at avoiding the mayhem that would sometimes occur as the 40 or more cars battled for money and position.

Soon they were out together, Cale and Betty Jo Thigpen, at the local drive-in and the movie theater.

Cale noticed that a particularly well-dressed man seemed to show up around their pits. He asked Joe Whitlock if he knew who the fellow was.

"That's Jacque Passino," Joe told him.

"Who's Jacque Passino?" Cale asked.

"Jacque Passino is Ford racing as far as I'm concerned," Joe answered.

"You mean like Ford factory?" Cale inquired.

"Exactly," Joe replied.

Cale became friendly with Jacque, and Jacque responded with parts for Cale's car. This relationship was working out well for a while, with Cale dreaming of working his way into a factory situation. Factory drivers made a good living at the track, and it is every driver's dream. Cale tried to impress Jacque every time he took to the track. Several races later they were at Richmond's dirt track. Cale had qualified 18th but had worked his way up through the pack to third when Little Joe Weatherly blew his engine while running just ahead. All the oil from the expired power plant fell to the track in front Cale's Ford. He had seen the oil hit the ground, so he braced himself, knowing what was ahead—Cale knew that the race car would lose all traction when it hit the oil and that he was headed toward the outside wall. As the car moved up the track, out of the racing groove, Cale sawed the wheel first one way, then the other, struggling to maintain any control of the hurtling machine. It was a losing battle. The Ford crashed into the outside retaining wall, and Cale knew by the impact that the car was no longer usable. He was unhurt, but all he could think about was whether or not he would still have Jacque's support. The Ford parts had improved his car immensely, and, even though he had not yet won a race, he felt his time was coming, and soon. The thoughts bothered him all night after the race, so the next morning Cale managed to summon the courage to call Jacque in Dearborn, Michigan, to find out for himself. Jacque was already aware of the crash and asked Cale how he was running before the crash. "Third," he replied. "That's good, Cale. Don't worry.

I'll help you. Just as long as you don't mess up. But if you do something stupid, that's the end of the parts," Jacque answered. Then he arranged for Herman to pick up a new body at Holman-Moody in Charlotte, the Ford factory operation. He also arranged for Herman to receive most of the major parts needed. Herman would need only to supply the incidentals. Cale had known within himself that he would become a top race car driver, and this help from the factory confirmed his feelings. The only thing better would have been a full factory ride, of which there were only a few.

Since his racing career was moving in the right direction, Cale decided it might be time to improve his life in other ways as well. He knew exactly what he needed to do, and he had been thinking for a while about it. He asked Betty Jo for her hand in marriage, and she accepted. She wondered aloud to Cale about his ability to support a family. Cale retorted, "I'm going to make it big in racing." She knew him well enough to know that he was dead serious. Then he pulled out a surprise and announced, "Until then, I'm going to make it big in the turkey business." Stunned, she replied, "The turkey business? Are you sure, Cale? I mean, turkeys?" Cale explained that he had been studying the turkey market, and that it could not miss. She accepted his answer, her faith in Cale solid. They would have to wait a while to tell her parents, until Cale could pull together some resources and begin to look as if he was serious about the turkey business. He went right to work, building a turkey house, covering the floor with wood shavings, as he had read. He bought a 10' by 50' mobile home, setting it up at the back of the farm near the turkey house. He knew that her parents wouldn't exactly approve of Betty Jo marrying a stock car driver, so he needed to show that he really meant to do well with the birds. They had already made the trip to the town office and secured their marriage license. Cale felt it best if she would tell her parents without his presence, so the plan was for him to pick her up after she had given them the news. They would then go to the preacher's house and be married that very evening. The butterflies in his stomach on the trip over to Hebron, where she lived, were not of the same species as the ones that he felt at the start of every race. These brought his heart to his throat, dried his mouth, and caused his mind to race as he tried to envision his future with the girl of his dreams. He arrived to find that Betty Jo was upset. Things had not gone well.

The Thigpens didn't care too much for the idea of the marriage, but they would find it easier to accept if they would have a church wedding with guests, a reception, and a proper ceremony. But Cale didn't want all that. The more they discussed the situation, the more frustrated he became. Betty Jo was caught in the trap of wanting to satisfy her parents and the man she loved, and there seemed no plausible answer. She became confused. Cale became so flustered that he announced, "Well, I know what I want. I want to leave. We'll wait a while or maybe we won't get married at all." He stomped out to his car and sped away, leaving a trail of thrown gravel. He drove around for over two hours, all the time turning his thoughts over and over in his head. He was mad, all right, and hurt, too. He finally decided that he didn't care what her parents wanted, this was what he wanted, and he was going to have it. He turned the car back in the direction of Hebron and made a dash for Betty Jo's house. He was going to carry away his bride, and he wasn't going to let anyone or anything stand in his way. They were both of age, and he was ready to face their challenge. As he neared, the dread of an ugly scene crept into his thoughts, but he shook it off, never even slowing down. As he approached their farm, he could see something at the head of the driveway. It was Betty Jo, with her suitcase, waiting for his return. He certainly had picked the right girl, as she was just like him. He loaded her suitcase into the car, and off they went to the preacher's house. The preacher had already left for another engagement, so they decided to just sit in his yard until he returned. He didn't get home

She wondered aloud to Cale about his ability to support a family. Cale retorted, "I'm going to make it big in racing."

until around midnight, and no one is sure what day they were married. It could have been April 7 or April 8, depending on what time the ceremony was completed, but the Yarboroughs still celebrate April 7 as their anniversary.

There was not much time for a honeymoon because Cale's first load of 5,000 turkeys was due to arrive the next afternoon. A quick drive to Charleston in the middle of the night, a stay in a little motel on the edge of town, and a morning drive around the city would have to suffice as a honeymoon, and they headed back toward home, where they were expecting the shipment. It was there waiting for them when they arrived. They unloaded the turkeys before they even unloaded the car. As the last of the turkeys found their way into the turkey house, Cale said, "Well, that oughta hold 'em 'til the morning, honey. Tonight we can get a good night's sleep in our own home." The trucker spoke up and shattered their plans when he told Cale, "I hate to tell you this, but someone is going to have to spend the night with the birds." "What do you mean, spend the night with the birds?" Betty Jo asked emphatically with her hands on her hips. "You can't leave them alone," the trucker explained. "The temperature has to be just right, and if it goes down too much, someone will have to close the doors and windows. If it gets too hot, you'll have to open it up. Someone is going to have to stay here." Their first full night of marriage was spent sleeping with 5,000 turkeys.

Cale had felt that the racetrack was no place for Betty Jo, so he had never taken her. Now that they were married, she began to show interest, probably because racing had such a hold on him. He knew she would be overwhelmed by a track like Daytona or Darlington, so he decided to take her to Columbia for her initiation. It all went well, and she enjoyed the race, even though she did not yet understand the protocol. The racing was progressing as normal, with Cale still finishing almost every race in the top 15. The parts from Ford certainly played a big part in his consistency. Then came the race at Darlington late in the season. Cale was running strong when a front wheel bearing failed, throwing him into the wall and out of the race. Jacque headed for the pits to find the problem. His deal with Herman was that Ford would supply the big parts, but they expected Herman to use the best parts he could find for the rest. He asked Herman where he had gotten the wheel bearing, and found that Herman had installed a used bearing. Jacque walked away, and so did Herman and Cale's deal with Ford. It was over as quickly as that.

With his ride now history, Cale had little to turn to but the turkeys. His logging business was in a coma, and the racetrack had nothing to offer, so his fate seemed to rest with 5,000 birds. Cale had never been so down. A few weeks later, the phone rang with an offer from a man in Charleston who wanted Cale to drive his car in a big race in Savannah. Cale was elated with the offer. The car was supposed to be a good one, so maybe this could lead to another chance. Also, the race paid well, and, at this point, the money could go a long way toward providing for the Yarboroughs and their turkeys. With only $10 in the bank, he and Betty Jo stopped to fill the car with gas on credit. They cashed a check for the $10 and headed for Savannah. Betty Jo had made some sandwiches, enough for the trip down and the ride home. They left in such a hurry that the sandwiches were left on their dining room table, but Cale promised her they would stop to eat on the way. After all, they still had $10. It began to rain, but the forecast called for clearing over the Georgia coast. The dirt track in Savannah would be a slippery one, and that knowledge gave Cale added confidence, as he knew he could handle such a track better than most. His daydream was rudely interrupted by the sound of a siren. As he looked into his rearview mirror, he saw the lights of a police car and pulled over. The officer had clocked him at 50 mph in a 45 mph zone and was unwilling to give Cale a break. Two choices were presented—either he could pay the officer on the spot or he could appear before the judge. There was no time for the judge, so Cale reached into his pocket and handed the officer the $10. It was the very last of their money, and Betty Jo was crying as they pulled from the curb to continue their trip.

The rest of the trip went without incident, but as they neared Savannah, Cale remembered that the bridge across the river required a 50¢ toll. "Do you have any money at all?" he asked his wife. "No" was the reply, as he explained the need for the toll. She climbed into the back seat and removed the cushions to look for change. There was 37¢ there, but they would still be 13¢ short. It seemed that Cale would miss the race over that 13¢. Cale kept driving, determined to make the race but unsure how. Luckily, when he reached the toll booth, traffic was light. When the attendant asked for the 50¢, Cale gave him the change they had found and began to explain his plight to the attendant. He accepted Cale's story, which was complete with the promise to pay the balance on the return trip. When the two finally reached the track, pit passes were going for $1 each. Cale happened to know the man at the gate and promised him the $2 as soon as he could find the car owner. Racers are always broke, so the man let him continue. They quickly found the car and owner and started the day with a $2.13 debt.

The car was a good one, and as Cale practiced in it, he had high hopes for the race. Betty Jo had found Lee Roy Yarbrough's wife and went over to sit with her and some of the other drivers' wives. It turned out to be a miserable time for her, as the other wives were constantly going to get something to eat, each time asking her if she would like something. Although she was starving, she would feign that she was stuffed to avoid the embarrassment of being completely broke. Things on the track turned ugly also, and when warming up for the first heat race, Cale blew the engine, ending his day. Cale knew the track promoter and went to him with his story. The promoter was kind enough to loan him $20 until the next race, so he ran to find Betty Jo. She was still in the grandstands with the other wives, acting as if all was well. Cale could tell as they walked to the car that she was almost in tears again when he asked her if she would like a hamburger. She thought it particularly cruel that he would ask such a question when they couldn't even afford to cross back over the bridge. Cale flashed the $20, and they headed for the nearest hamburger joint.

As they reached the toll bridge, traffic was rather heavy. When Cale pulled up to the booth, he paid the 50¢ toll, then gave the attendant the 13¢ that he owed. "I owe this to Buford over there from my trip before. Would you see that he gets it?" he asked. The attendant responded, but in such a way as to give some doubt that the task would be completed. "You can give it to him now," Cale said. The attendant balked because of the growing line of traffic. Cale shut off his car and said he would wait. Finally, the attendant figured the quickest resolution would be to give the money to Buford. Buford waved to Cale, so off toward home they went. Cale could never cross that toll bridge again without stopping for a minute to talk with Buford, their newfound friend.

Cale reached home that night in as low a state as he had ever experienced. He was broke, and there seemed to be dark, heavy clouds over his future. Maybe he had chosen the wrong path. Perhaps being a part-time logger, part-time turkey farmer, part-time semipro football player, and part-time racer would not fulfill his dreams. It surely wasn't putting money in his pocket the way he wanted. So he decided the thing to do was to retire from racing. He announced his retirement, and the newspapers all over the South ran the story. Phone calls came from all over, with loyal fans and supporters trying to change his mind. Cale was steadfast, though, politely letting them know that the decision had been made. He decided to spend his time concentrating on the logging and turkey businesses, determined to make each successful. He had no choice. Betty Jo had revealed that she was pregnant, so now there would be another mouth to feed and more responsibilities. Cale really buckled down, went to work, and proceeded with his new plan.

Cale reached home that night in as low a state as he had ever experienced. He was broke, and there seemed to be dark, heavy clouds over his future. Maybe he had chosen the wrong path.

The phone rang one afternoon shortly thereafter. It was Jacque Passino, the Ford man who had helped until Herman had breached the deal. Jacque started the conversation by talking to Cale about his new plans, sounding like another well-wisher. Then he asked, "What are you really going to do, Cale?" Cale explained from his heart that he was going to log and raise turkeys, but what he would really like to do was race. He just had no car, and racing was not paying the bills. Also, his family was about to expand, and he was excited and anxious about that. Jacque then offered Cale a chance to try out as a driver for the Holman-Moody race team in Charlotte. Fred Lorenzen was their primary driver, but they had decided to enter a second car and would need a driver for the new team. They had chosen two to try out for the job, and Cale was one of them. The other driver was a guy from Michigan named Benny Parsons. Cale could not believe his ears. Holman-Moody was the Ford factory-sponsored team, the team where Ned Jarrett, Fireball Roberts, and David Pearson had honed their skills. With the best talent, equipment, and facilities available at the time, Holman-Moody had a longstanding reputation for building the best cars and the best drivers in the business. Immediately, Cale's new plan was put on hold. He could not pass up an offer like this, even though the thrill of the opportunity could not completely wipe out his memories of the bad luck and disappointment the racetrack often left him with. He told Jacque he would be at the Holman-Moody shop first thing the next morning to be fitted for a seat.

Cale was to try out in Weaverville, near Asheville. The familiar butterflies were out in force as he sat on the starting line that night. This could be his big chance. A good showing on this night could change his life, and he knew it. Nonetheless, they had sought him out, so the best idea seemed to be to go out there and run the race as he normally would. That's what had attracted them to start with. He qualified the #00 Ford in the fifth spot, and when the green flag fell, he started strong. As a matter of fact, he ran strong for most of the race, battling with the legends for the top spot. He was driving like a pro, like a Holman-Moody driver is expected to drive. Then, as luck would have it, on Lap 267, the car ahead ran over a large piece of debris on the track, and it bounced straight into Cale's radiator, relieving it of all its coolant and ending his night. At this point, Cale was very glad that he had not discarded his memories of disappointment. It would help him cope with the current situation. Even though the DNF had not been his fault, he felt his chance for the factory ride had all but disappeared. He found John Holman in the pits, and said, "If it weren't for bad luck, I'd have no luck at all, John." But John replied, "It's not as bad as you think, Cale. You did a damn fine job out there, and it wasn't any fault of yours that you didn't win that race. We're giving you the ride."

There were only five more races in the 1964 season, and Cale contested them for the Holman-Moody team. What an operation he had joined! They had a race hauler for the car, a real pit crew, and all kinds of new parts. The last five races would serve as a little warm-up for the '65 season.

As Betty Jo's pregnancy progressed, Cale usually drove to the tracks alone, often returning the same night as the race. Such was the case the night of the Norfolk race. Cale needed to return home for a turkey deal he had made for the next morning. He brokered his flock through General Mills, and they had found a buyer for 5,000 turkeys. His flock had grown to over 10,000 by this time, but not all were ready for market. He drove home through the night, arriving in the morning. About an hour later, the truck showed up to load for his journey to New York. They had just began to load the turkeys when Betty Jo called for Cale. It became quite apparent that the time had come to go to the hospital for the delivery. Now! Cale had no idea what to do. "Cale, I know you can't go right now," Betty Jo told him. "I'll be all right. I can drive myself to the hospital, and you can come as soon as you are finished." Lady Luck may not have followed Cale to the racetrack every time, but when he found Betty Jo, she had certainly been watching over him. The men finished loading the turkeys into the truck, and the driver handed Cale a receipt for them. Standard procedure was that the turkeys would arrive at market, then Cale would receive a check. He sent the turkeys on their way, then headed to the hospital. It had only been a couple hours since Betty Jo had left, but when Cale arrived, he found that he had a new daughter, Julie Ann. She was absolutely beautiful! Cale was happier than if he had won the race at Darlington.

Betty Jo and Julie came home from the hospital three days later. The 5,000 turkeys arrived back at Cale's farm on the same day. The trip to New York had gone well, but when they had arrived, the shipment had been refused due to a surprise drop in prices. By this time, the birds were in sore shape, having been without food or water for three days. Soon Cale had the task of having thousands of dead turkeys to bury. He dug trenches with the tractor where he could push the carcasses, but the mid-September heat ensured that the odor was intense and long-lasting. It was the end of the turkey business for Cale. He had earned over $10,000 in the '64 racing season, and with the new ride, he did not need the income from the turkeys like he once did. Besides, with setbacks like the one he had just had, profit would have been just a vision on the horizon.

About a week later, at the race shop, John Holman approached Cale. "I'm really sorry, Cale," he said. "I'll guarantee you, it's nothing you did. You did a real good job for us. Ford just decided not to race the extra car next year and, well, you understand, my other drivers have been with me a long time."

Once more, Cale boarded the emotional roller coaster that seemed to be the pattern of his life. The hurt was obvious, and John put his arm around Cale's shoulder to be of comfort. "I'll tell you what," he said. "You can come and work for me at the shop, you know, just doing odd jobs, and maybe something will turn up. You know, it's not the worst place in the world for a race car driver to hang around. If something does turn up, you'll be the first one to know about it. We won't have to look for you." It sounded like a good idea, but what would Betty Jo think?

"I'll let you know tomorrow, I have to talk to Betty Jo first," he told John.

As Cale considered all that John had just revealed, his mind ran circles around itself. What should he do? It seemed that all that he had been counting on had suddenly evaporated. Here he was with a wife and daughter to support and no immediate means of income. Lesser men would just give up, maybe turn to drinking over such a dilemma. But Cale had never fit in that category. He had listened to John's offer, and even though the pay was a meager $1.25 per hour, he would be right in the middle of the racing world, the world he loved. He had all the confidence in the world that, if given the chance, he could prove himself. He remembered his childhood goal of being a NASCAR star, a dream that had never diminished in its focus, and decided that this was the next step toward that goal. Besides, his turkey experience had whetted his appetite for farming for the moment.

His explanation to Betty Jo was accepted as the logical direction for Cale to turn. Even with Cale's talents, he felt he had little chance of becoming a star driver as a journeyman, driving whatever ride was available on a given night. He needed an alliance with a team that was as good as he was. Holman-Moody had been that sort of team, but it wasn't the only one out there. John had pretty much told him that he was next in line, and connections like John Holman were not easy to come by.

Fifty dollars a week didn't allow for much luxury in Charlotte. Two dollars a night bought a room at one of the motels near the airport. Holman and Moody's shop was a decent place to work, the job was pretty easy, and he was around race cars all day. All sorts of important and interesting people came through the doors, so Cale really was in the forefront of the sport.

Bernard Alvarez had a new Ford he wanted to race at Daytona, and Cale was able to convince him to let him pilot it. It was a Ford, and maybe he could do well, impressing the Holman and Moody group. The format at Daytona is a little different in that there is also a 100-mile qualifying race in addition to the regular qualifying. Cale started the qualifier strong. The Ford felt good, and the engine powerful. As the laps counted off, he moved toward the front of the field. He was racing another car hard, keeping the inside lane, when the outside car hit the wall. Cale saw it happening, swinging his car sideways on purpose to avoid the debris strewn in front of him. If he could slide down on the grassy infield portion of the track, he could bring the car under control without hitting anything, find his way back to the track, and continue. There were still plenty of laps left to win this race. All of a sudden there was a terrific explosion inside the car. It was as if both right tires had blown at exactly the same time. Sliding through the infield, it wasn't until he stopped that he realized what had happened. The complete front wheel assembly of the damaged car—brakes, suspension, and all—had come

Cale was still in driving position, not even aware that the steering wheel had been torn from his hands.

through the right side of Cale's car at the A-pillar, wiping out the entire dashboard, steering wheel, and steering column. Cale was still in driving position, not even aware that the steering wheel had been torn from his hands. As he came to his senses, the shock short-lived, it was one of those wrecks that Cale considered to be a good wreck. That is, a wreck that he could walk away from, still intact. That wheel assembly, if it had hit just one foot farther back, would have taken off his head for sure.

After Daytona, there was enough money to afford a small apartment in Charlotte. Finally, Cale could have his family with him again. The job at Holman and Moody was getting easier for him to take, as he was now getting to take some of the race cars they were building to the airport to shake them down. The people he was meeting there were offering more racing opportunities, especially in the sportsman classes. Even though some of the races were as far away as Georgia and Alabama, Cale, Betty Jo, and Julie would all climb into the car for the road trip. Sometimes they would sleep in the car, but the separation until they had gotten the apartment had been enough for a while.

Cale may have been pretty busy racing in the sportsman classes, but still there were no Grand National opportunities. Sometimes this would give Cale doubt that he would ever make it big like he had always thought he would. Some of his old friends were already fairly deep in Grand National experience. Lee Roy Yarbrough already had taken two checkered flags, and his old traveling buddy Tiny Lund had won one. Would he be able to catch up with them?

Two things happened to improve matters. First, John Holman had a fishing cabin on the Catawba River not too far from the shop, and he offered to give it to Cale and Betty Jo to live in. It needed a little help, with a leaky roof, dingy paint, broken windows, and missing screens. But the Yarboroughs saw a diamond in the rough, accepted the offer, and began to do the repairs. The $60 a month they were saving from the apartment rent helped their meager budget, and before too long they had a pretty little cottage by the river. Second, John had decided to pull out one of the cars from the year before and give Cale a Grand National ride. Red Myler was hired to maintain the car at his shop, but Holman and Moody would supply all the parts. The car would be fairly competitive, and it offered Cale another opportunity to show his skills. He was determined to make the best impression possible at every event. The plan was for Cale to run all 54 races in the 1965 season, so he could use this season to prove to the top owners that he was worthy of one of their rides.

The season started rocky, with a crash at Daytona. Through 12 races, Cale had only finished three, with all the rest ending early because of mechanical failure or crashes. The three races he had finished had turned out all right, including third and ninth place finishes. At the Columbia race, Cale led three laps, the first laps he had led in Grand National. The weekly races helped to increase his feel for the car, and he was beginning to move up in the field. He was also becoming more familiar with the other drivers, their habits and racing styles, and also their weaknesses. His hard-charging style would cause him to drive over his head at times, but he was getting better at getting himself out of trouble and avoiding crashes.

The race at Valdosta coincided with some testing he was doing for the Holman and Moody team at

Charlotte. Ralph Moody was going to fly Cale to Valdosta for the race, as this was the only way he could be at both places on schedule. The weather turned sour, canceling the flight. As a result, Sam McQuagg qualified the car and placed in the middle of the pack. Cale was worried that he would miss the race altogether, but the weather moved south and postponed the race until the next day. With the extra 24 hours, Cale loaded Betty Jo and Julie in the car and headed for Valdosta.

Valdosta was a half-mile dirt track, just like those Cale had cut his racing teeth on. He was immediately at home on the track and plowed through the field to the front. All the big boys were in the race, but Cale had whipped them before, and he was doing it again. He had seen his share of adversity, though, so he never even thought of winning. *Just take it smooth, and finish*, he told himself. As the race progressed, he was still out front, with few serious challengers. With 10 laps to go, there was a spin in front of him, and he barely made contact with the spinning car's bumper, sending his car sideways. Cale sawed the steering wheel to take advantage of the slide through the turn, straightened the car without losing too much ground, and continued to charge forward. Buddy Baker moved up to challenge, and the two were running side by side through Turn 1. There was not enough room for the two cars, and the sides of their cars came together in a shower of sparks. They both exited the turn in the same position. Cale pulled ahead on the back straight-away and pulled to the inside, slamming the door on his opponent. Coming out of Turn 4 down the front straight, he noticed that the flagman was waving the white flag. There was just one more lap, just four more turns, and he would have his first Grand National victory. That last half-mile seemed as if it were 10 miles long, and it felt as if every car on the track was loose and headed right for him. He stayed high on the track, avoiding any troubles, made a good run off of Turn 4, and took the checkered flag.

It was the sweetest victory lap he had ever taken, waving the checkered flag to the fans

Cale pulled ahead on the back straight-away and pulled to the inside, slamming the door on his opponent.

out the window, with a grin on his face that might never leave. He wanted to kiss Betty Jo. He wanted to kiss the world. In an instant, he had finished an apprenticeship that had lasted for almost 80 races. It had been quite a long and bumpy road, but it had been worth it to Cale.

The next week at the Firecracker 500 in Daytona, his confidence was busting out all over. Always a hard qualifier, he started the race from the second row on the inside. Marvin Panch had qualified first for the Wood brothers, and Earl Balmer lined up beside him on the front row. It was only several laps until Cale had grabbed the lead. He was ahead of the best in the world—A.J. Foyt, Junior Johnson, Fred Lorenzen, and the rest were lined up behind him like a freight train. He was proud to be ahead of the number one Holman and Moody car, driven by Lorenzen, but even prouder to be ahead of Foyt, whom Cale had always admired. Foyt had driven everything with wheels on it, from dirt track to Indy, and had been successful at all of them.

Lap after lap, Cale stayed ahead of the field. He led 72 of the first 108 laps, then the engine decided it could take no more and blew. Cale could have been disappointed, but he knew that people would remember his name. He had led the best racers in the world around the premier racetrack in the world. Oh yeah, people would remember his name.

Only a few weeks later, Ford arranged for Cale to drive for Banjo Matthews. Banjo's lead driver, Bobby Johns, had decided to try Indy car racing, leaving an empty seat for the upcoming Charlotte race. Cale would fill in for him. Cale took advantage of the opportunity, qualifying the car on the outside of the front row, then led more than 20 laps before the engine called it a day. He had run the car hard, and Matthews was impressed. Johns returned from Indy to run for Banjo at the Atlanta race the next week, but after the event, Banjo gave the ride to Cale permanently. Obviously he had seen something he liked a lot in Charlotte.

The Ford Banjo screwed together was a racing instrument. He had been a racer himself for many years, winning many times. He knew what was demanded of a race car and built his cars to win. It was the first time Cale truly had a first-class ride. Beyond the car, Cale and Banjo formed a close relationship. Banjo shared some of his racing secrets and coached Cale at the different tracks. They formed an understanding of each other, and Banjo could transform wishes and needs into mechanical credibility. Together, they looked toward a bright future. It certainly would not be easy, though. Every week they would have to compete against drivers like Richard Petty, Ned Jarrett, Curtis Turner, and Junior Johnson. Each of them would be fielding cars equal to theirs.

It was the first time Cale truly had a first-class ride.

Driving the entire Grand National schedule was grueling, but 1965 had been a good year for Cale. Of the 46 races he contested, he had his first win, finished in the top 10 21 times, 13 of those top fives. He had qualified second several times but had yet to crack the pole position. He had also won more than $24,000. He had already bought a nicer house on Lake Wylie, and things were looking up. He was traveling much more, though, and the more he was welcomed into the daily lives of the other drivers, the less he appreciated the track as a suitable place for his wife and daughter. He would be away from home for stretches as long as two weeks, and Betty Jo was getting a little homesick for South Carolina. Cale missed the sandy fields and mossy trees as well, so they bought a two-story columned white house in Timmonsville. Cale had more extra money than ever, so he began investing in land around the area. He had always dreamed of owning a 1,000-acre spread, so he found a 500-acre parcel near Sardis. It would serve as a good start.

Shenanigans of all sorts happened at or near the track as the individual personalities of each of the drivers could only be held in check for short periods of time. Little Joe Weatherly seemed to be in the middle of many of the pranks and practical jokes, and had been dubbed "the Clown Prince of Racing." At Darlington, he had tossed a rubber snake into several of the drivers' cars, including Cale's. It was enough to scare some of the drivers from their cars. Little Joe would roll around on the ground laughing. That night, Cale went home from the track and went snake hunting. Sure enough, he was able to find a rattlesnake, which he carefully trapped with a forked stick, put in a burlap sack, and carried home. He carefully removed the animal's fangs and took the burlap bag to the track the next day. When he arrived, he found Little Joe in his race car, so he walked over, bent down, removed the snake from its sack, and tossed it through the window into Little Joe's lap. Little Joe looked down, and his eyes grew as big as dinner plates. The look on his face said, "What the…?" and he froze as the snake emitted its familiar rattle. If there were such a record for removing belts and exiting the car, he would have beat it. Leaping from the car, as white as a ghost, he found a hammer and began chasing Cale. He chased him with such dedication that Cale knew he had better leave and let him cool down a little. If Little Joe caught him, he might kill him. All said and done, Little Joe never touched a rubber snake again in his life, much less brought one to the track.

One day at the Charlotte track, Cale and Banjo were testing some Firestone tires. At lunchtime, they all decided to head for a barbeque house not too far from the track. There were two rental cars for their transport, so Banjo and Cale jumped into a Ford and the Firestone engineer took the Chevy. There was always a race to lunch and back, and this day was no different. After lunch, they headed back to the speed-way with their pedals pushed to the floor. They would always race back to the double tunnel that led to the infield. The first to the tunnel would win. On this day, as they approached the tunnel, they were running neck-and-neck. Neither man wanted to lift, and they both entered the tunnel at the same time. The tunnel would barely handle two cars wide, and, upon exit, narrowed even further with an uphill exit that led to an immediate right turn into the pits. Both cars made the right turn, banging against each other time after time. Banjo was headed straight for a telephone pole but didn't flinch. Cale yelled at him time and again about the pole, but it didn't matter, it was full steam ahead. The impact threw both Banjo and Cale from the Ford, whose accelerator stuck, sending it into the Chevy. Both cars ended up in a fence. Cale picked himself up, dusted off, and took inventory of all his parts. Everything was still there, then he looked over at Banjo. He was all bloody, and his glasses were hanging from one ear.

"I told you we were going to hit that pole," Cale reminded Banjo.

"What pole?" was the full answer.

After caring for Banjo's wounds, they called Hertz, asking for another car.

"What's wrong with the one you have?" asked the rental clerk.

Banjo replied, "The radiator's leaking."

"What happened?" the clerk inquired.

"I don't know. It just stopped," was Banjo's reply.

You would think that a rental company would know enough not to rent cars to racers.

CHAPTER 5

The Champion

Nascar was started in 1948 by Bill France Sr. as a sincere attempt to homologate rules for stock-car racing. France had recognized the gaining popularity of such racing throughout the South after World War II. Many of the troops had returned from Europe and the Pacific Rim to a country that had been so involved in banding together for national protection that the entertainment industry for the general population was in somewhat of a slump. The opportunity was ripe for the creation of a new entertainment venue to attract the everyday working man. America was a mechanical society, and the automobile had become an integral part of the American way. In almost every town of any size, someone seized the opportunity, building dirt tracks to promote the competition of car against car for the entertainment of the masses.

These tracks were often fairly crude, generally requiring a field, a man with a tractor, and the building of some sort of seating. Rarely was there much design work involved, and the quality of the track depended on the skill of the tractor operator. Most times the tracks operated independently, creating their own rules and enforcing those rules according to their own specific whims. As the popularity of the sport began to grow, there was a certain amount of frustration among the racing community. A car suited to the rules of one track might not be eligible to compete at another, and the loosely knit system of rules and regulations meant that each race stood on its own merit. Each time a racer would compete, it was a new day.

France had the idea that, if he could band together a series of races under the same umbrella of rules, there was an opportunity to create situations like those in the organized "ball" sports. Just as home teams in professional sports attract and maintain a fan base loyal to the team all year, he felt it was possible to gather the same sort of fan loyalty in stock-car racing. The first races he organized encouraged him to continue his efforts. He was a smart businessman and surrounded himself with people whose ideas he respected. With a flair for promotion like P.T. Barnum, his innovative approach to the presentation of his events brought almost immediate attention. Other forward-thinking men in the South watched his success and found ways to jump on the bandwagon for a share of the money NASCAR was beginning to

William Caleb "Cale" Yarborough was born on March 27, 1940 in Timmonsville, South Carolina. PHOTO COURTESY OF CALE YARBOROUGH.

As a teenager, Cale worked after school at Gregory's Tobacco Warehouse in order to pay for his 1930 Ford Model A coupe. PHOTO COURTESY OF CALE YARBOROUGH.

Betty Jo, Cale, and their three daughters enjoy a Christmas at home. PHOTO COURTESY OF CALE YARBOROUGH.

Cale captures the pole at Daytona in 1970 with a one-lap-speed of 194.015.

Cale Yarborough and then-presidential candidate Jimmy Carter at Darlington in 1976.

Posing in victory lane after winning the American 500 at Rockingham in 1978.

Another day, another trophy—this time at the 1979 Coca-Cola 500 at Pocono.

Cale and team owner Junior Johnson pause for a photo at Talladega in 1978.

Cale's #11 car collides with Donnie Allison on the final lap of the 1979 Daytona 500…

…which led to a post-race scuffle between Allison's brother Bobby and Cale.

Victory at Daytona! In 1984, Cale had the fastest qualifying time, won a qualifying race, and then the 500, a feat never before accomplished.

Cale celebrates his Daytona victory with a champagne shower.

The happy couple: Betty Jo and Cale Yarborough. PHOTO COURTESY OF CALE YARBOROUGH.

generate. Each year, the list of tracks that hosted NASCAR events grew, and the number of races increased accordingly. A respected infrastructure helped the series gain popularity, and often the tracks would be filled to capacity with spectators hungry for the kinds of action found at the racetrack.

As the crowds grew, so did the revenue. With a little prodding, asphalt tracks began to pop up. Darlington was one of the first—a one-and-a-half-mile oval with banked turns, designed to appeal to both the racers and the fans. Instead of building to accommodate a few thousand fans, these new tracks were built to attract tens of thousands. And attract them they did. A typical race weekend would literally increase the population of an area, filling motels and restaurants near the tracks. The influx of money made the tracks good investments, and the local governments welcomed the opportunity to capitalize on this newfound source of funding. Each new track that rose up from the countryside would try to better the last. Each was different in layout, surface, accommodations, and concessions. The seating allowed better views of the action, sometimes allowing fans a view of the entire track.

Just 10 years after its inception, NASCAR had woven itself into the very fabric of Southern life. Tobacco, cotton, textiles, and NASCAR held equal status as Southern staples. The media had picked up on the sensation, and drivers began to have followings, people who cheered them on specifically and faithfully. Local newspapers would all report race results, and race fans throughout the South could follow their favorites from week to week, sharing the joy of victories and the disappointment of lesser results.

Tracks measuring at least one-and-a-half miles in length were built in Darlington, Daytona, Charlotte, and Atlanta. They became dubbed "superspeedways," as their length and relatively smooth racing surfaces allowed for greater and greater speeds. Whereas on a half-mile dirt track a driver might struggle to run 100 mph to 120 mph, on the superspeedways, speeds of over 170 mph were needed just to qualify for a race. As speeds increased, so did the fan base. Almost from the time they were erected, tracks continually added to their capacities, a process that continues today.

Tobacco, cotton, textiles, and NASCAR held equal status as Southern staples.

Since the first lap Cale drove in Daytona in 1962, he had felt at ease on the superspeedways. Whether it was his daredevil temperament, desire to wring every mile-per-hour out of his car, or just natural ability to see the correct line around the track, he had always been able to run his best when the fastest speeds were involved. Maybe it was just serendipitous that Cale's learning curve and the development of these arenas fit hand-in-hand. Whatever the reasoning, it was obvious that he was a force to be reckoned with anytime he was entered to race at one of these speed-fests. Running at one of these longer tracks required a completely different style of driving, and all the drivers were learning together. Temperatures in the cars would often reach upwards of 140 degrees, retarding concentration and endurance. Some were adapting better than others, and Cale was picking it up faster than anyone.

Higher speeds cause greater crashes, the kind more likely to end a driver's career or even take his life. The threat of peril at the superspeedways was always indiscriminate, not caring about a driver's experience. Accidents at great speeds allow little time for reaction, sometimes leading to multicar pileups. Unfortunately, it is the drivers from behind who are not at fault that most often suffer the greatest consequences. Nineteen sixty-four was a particularly tragic year, as Little Joe Weatherly, the Clown Prince of Racing, was killed when he slammed into the wall at Riverside. The Charlotte race was the scene of a horrific accident that took the life of Fireball Roberts, who was probably as good on the long tracks as anybody. Any death on the track had a rippling effect on the rest of the drivers. As the drivers were a closely knit group, each was the loss of a close friend. Usually each driver would get an up-close view of the scene of a crash, wondering if the driver made it through. Some could erect a mental block until the race was over, continuing to race as hard as before. Little Joe's death was the first to really affect Cale. They had raced together for many years, and he was truly a great friend. Cale learned that to be successful in the car, he had to remain stoic behind the wheel. It wasn't that it didn't matter, or that he didn't care, it was just that, as he figured, any loss of concentration for any reason increased the chances of him following in Little Joe's footsteps.

It was four months later at Charlotte when, on Lap 7, Junior Johnson lost traction in Turn 2 and swung his car sideways, directly into the paths of Ned Jarrett and Fireball Roberts. They were running side by side just behind Junior, too close to avoid a collision. Both hit Junior's car in the side, and Fireball's Ford careened down to the inside, concrete retaining wall. The car met the wall hard, and the gas tank exploded. Flames engulfed the entire area. Ned had jumped from his car and tried to get Fireball out, but the fire was too much. Cale watched on the next yellow lap as they pulled Fireball, who was not moving, from his car. For each of the next several laps, the car was there as Cale entered the backstretch, but finally he came around and the track was empty. It was much easier to suppress the thoughts about the crash without having to look at it on every revolution of the track. Of course, as soon as the checkered flag waved, all thoughts returned to Fireball. Cale was informed of the gravity of the crash the minute he returned to the pits.

Insulation from disaster became an important ingredient in the recipe for a champion driver. Davey MacDonald and Eddie Sachs were killed at Indy, but Indy was a different ballgame, so the effects of their deaths were heartfelt but minimally affected Cale's driving. Jimmy Pardue and Billy Wade were both killed testing tires, and Cale was not there, so he didn't have to witness their crashes—he could remove himself from them also. Some drivers began to wonder if stock-car racing represented some sort of death wish, but that thought never entered Cale's reasoning. He was confident enough in his own abilities that he had made himself truly believe that it could not happen to him. Perhaps the fact that he had lost his father at such a tender age helped him to cope with loss after loss of these close friends.

Darlington, 1965, was proof that Cale learned from his mistakes. Cale brought the Ford through Turn 1 as fast as the car could stand before breaking traction and came up fast on Sam McQuagg's #24 Ford. The racing groove on that end of the track was very narrow, and passing another car through Turns 1 and 2 was always a treacherous proposition. Cale felt he had enough momentum to swing around McQuagg and be gone. He squeezed his car below the orange #24, and they touched. There just wasn't enough room for two cars to get around at speed. The contact between the two loosened Cale's car's grip, and the 150 mph–plus wind under his car lifted it from the track, propelling it over Sam's car. Cale's view was the strangest he had ever seen from the cockpit of a race car. As if in slow motion, he watched the orange Ford pass beneath him. All he could see was the green grass beneath him as he flew upside down. The normally raucous atmosphere inside the cockpit became eerily quiet, with the wind the predominate sound. If it was green beneath him, then he was no longer on the racetrack, but over the fence and over the parking lot. The banking in Turn 2 meant that it would be at least a 50-foot drop to the ground, so Cale braced himself for the upcoming impact. Flight had distorted time, extending what was seconds into what seemed like hours. There was time for Cale to wonder about the integrity of the car and to compare his situation to that of an astronaut. He wondered what Banjo's reaction to his demolition would be. All the while he was in the air, he was still driving the car. Turning the steering wheel and mashing the brakes had no effect, but it was just a natural reflex to try to maintain control. The quiet turned to chaos as the car came to earth. The shrill screech of twisting metal and the profound rumble of mass meeting ground echoed off the earthen bank defining the

Some drivers began to wonder if stock-car racing represented some sort of death wish, but that thought never entered Cale's reasoning.

outside of the track. The jolt could be felt in every bone and nerve of Cale's being. Instant pain consumed him from head to toe as his tensed body succumbed to the landing. He reached down, unbuckled his seatbelt, and propelled himself from the driver's window, unsure of fire. He was sitting on the bank, and Joe Whitlock was the first to arrive on the scene. Stunned to find Cale all in one piece, all he could do was start laughing. It was the best aerial show Darlington had ever seen.

Even before his first victory, Cale had already become quite respected for his track abilities. He had proven a certain dirt-track prowess developed from his earliest experiences at the outlaw tracks around his home, then refined in Sportsman, Modified, and Grand National competition throughout the South. Whether running qualifying laps or in the heart of a 500-lap main event, he had learned to get himself tuned into the race car. It was almost as if he and the car could communicate with each other to find the right mix of throttle and steering to reveal the limit of performance. If another driver could outrun Cale, it was because their equipment was better suited to the task at hand, not because they were driving harder.

Race cars built and fielded by Banjo Matthews were the cream of the crop. They were built to win, not just to compete. In the early NASCAR years, only a handful of car builders had kept on the leading edge, continuously exploring new options and developing specialized parts. Banjo was one of those builders, and the spirit of competition among these teams was fierce. The combination of good equipment and Cale's determination and talent was already yielding results. The wins only put icing on the cake. Qualifying positions were becoming consistently better and better. Starting a race at the front of the field was a huge advantage, as there was less traffic to negotiate and the chance of getting caught up in a crash was greatly diminished. Top 10 finishes were becoming commonplace, and for the first time in his Grand National career, Cale was earning championship points worth paying attention to. He had finished the 1965 season 10th in points, up from 19th in 1964.

Some were adapting better than others, and Cale was picking it up faster than anyone.

Manufacturers had become heavily involved in NASCAR by the mid-1960s, spending big dollars on research and development of new models to send to the racetrack. Chrysler gained somewhat of a lead with their Hemi engine. It was unbeatable unless it broke or crashed. The Plymouths and Dodges were winning everything, and the situation became so lopsided that Ford complained to NASCAR that something needed to be done to even the playing field. The response from NASCAR, or the lack of it, resulted in Ford pulling out of the competition. Of course, this meant Cale lost the Banjo Matthews ride just seven races into the 1966 season. He had always admired A.J. Foyt and Dan Gurney, and had often wondered how well he would compete in Indy. It seemed the ideal time to find out.

Driving at Indy and driving in NASCAR are only comparable in that the cars all have four wheels and a steering wheel. While a stock car of the mid-1960s weighed in at almost two tons, an open-wheel Indy car weighed only 1,600 pounds. Open cockpits allowed complete airflow to the driver, which could be a blessing and a nuisance at the same time. The track had been built in 1909 as the ultimate racing circuit of its type in the world. At two-and-a-half miles in length, with long straights front and back, speeds topping 200 mph were reached twice each lap. If a stock car is a butter knife, then an Indy car is a surgical scalpel, so precise and accurate through the controls that great care must be taken not to exaggerate input. Steering only required about an inch of movement to negotiate the turns, aided by fancy footwork with the throttle to control traction. Brakes were so powerful that they were best left alone. The slightest touch of the brake pedal at speed could throw the car into a 200-mph slide toward the wall. The gyrotic effect of airflow from the open wheels had the effect of magnetism, bringing cars closer together. Unlike in stock cars, where beating and banging is considered normal racing, if the open wheels of two cars met, the rotation of the lead car's tires could catapult the following car into the air. The result was never conducive to winning. Banking was absent in the turns, so their negotiation had to be attacked in a completely different manner than the high-banked turns at the NASCAR tracks.

Only two drivers had been able to make the adjustment to succeed in both Indy and NASCAR—Paul Goldsmith and A.J. Foyt. Dan Gurney came from Indy to NASCAR, but he ran the road course at Riverside, and road racing had been his apprenticeship. Others had tried, but with limited success. Bobby Johns had finished seventh at Indy, but came back to NASCAR after only one year. Marshall Teague tried several times, making it twice, and finished seventh in 1957. He was killed in a crash at Daytona while testing a speedway car. Junior Johnson, Curtis Turner, and Lee Roy Yarbrough had given it a shot, but none made the race. None of that meant anything to Cale. He had to give it a try. He was sure he could make the crossover. He could drive anything with wheels on it. He had made enough money in the '65 NASCAR season to keep the family secure while he gave it a try.

Cale arranged a trip to Indy, where he met his good friend A.J. Foyt. A.J. introduced Cale to the track, walking the pits and front stretch, and driving him around in a pace car, explaining the preferred racing lines and pointing out key points to a successful lap.

Lloyd Ruby quickly became a friend of Cale's, giving him insight on the track and on speedway racing as a whole.

The atmosphere at the track was a completely new experience for Cale. He was used to almost a family atmosphere within NASCAR, where each of the drivers was eager to help the other at the track, and time away from the track was usually spent together. That sense of brotherhood seemed missing at Indy. Perhaps it was because of the limited racing schedule of the speedway series, but there was an aloof feeling among the drivers. They were friendly enough, they just didn't get too close to each other. In NASCAR, the drivers raced together up to 50 times a year, with the time spent at the different tracks far outweighing their time at home with their wives and families. But Cale had come to Indy as a racer, not a politician, so he focused on the task at hand.

He found a ride in the red and yellow #66 Jim Robbins Special, a rear-engined Ford-powered car built by Rolla Vollstedt. One of the first cars on the track for practice, Cale had to pass the driver's test strictly adhered to by the officials. The first few laps are run at perhaps 120 mph, then as the laps progress, so do the speeds, until the car is running full-song. With the 200-mph straights, the officials needed to be sure that each driver had the skills to compete at this level. Cale aced the test with an almost perfect score.

Cale immediately liked the speedway car. He sat low to the ground, and the car fit around him as if it was tailored for him. All the controls were handy to reach, precise in their action. The car felt as if it was made from one piece of metal instead of a collection of parts. The quick touch of a control brought instant results, requiring complete concentration. The wind over his head gave the sensation of speed, feeding Cale's adrenaline. Activities preceding Indy last for about a month, so there is plenty of time to run laps. Cale spent as much time on the track as possible, feeling more confident, first, that he could compete, and, second, that he could win the race. He had become intimate with both the car and track. He qualified the car 24th, but some of his practice times had bettered the qualifying speeds of Mario Andretti and Jimmy Clark, who had qualified on the front row.

> **The wind over his head gave the sensation of speed, feeding Cale's adrenaline.**

Unfortunately, fate was once again unkind to Cale. As soon as the green flag dropped, he pushed the throttle to the floor. Just ahead of him, Billy Foster, who had qualified 12th also driving a Vollstedt/Ford for Jim Robbins, got sideways and bounced off the outside wall back across the track. There was a chain reaction of cars spinning, slamming into each other, bouncing apart, and sending wheels and axles flying through the air. At least a dozen cars were involved, including Cale's #66. He was hit from the side, then another car slammed into his rear. One of the flying wheels came down in his windshield area, rendering the car useless for the rest of the day. It had been a grand attempt, yet he couldn't even complete one lap. If he was to ever show his stuff on a speedway track, it would have to wait for another day.

Back home in NASCAR, the politics had stabilized and the atmosphere was back to normal. Cale had missed 30 races, but was still able to land a ride with the legendary Wood Brothers race team. They used the last five races of the season to get to know each other, to fit the hand into the glove, so to speak. Marion Cox had given Cale his first ride on short tracks, Herman Beam had taught him how to be a winner on the short tracks, Holman and Moody had offered the connection to a Grand National ride, and Banjo Matthews had taught him how to compete at the top level. If you could compare his experiences to a college education, he now had his master's degree, and the Wood Brothers team offered him the chance to earn his doctorate. There were five Wood brothers—Glen, Leonard, Delano, Clay, and Ray Lee—from Stuart, Virginia. Glen and Leonard concentrated on the building of the cars and engines, and the other brothers served the team as mechanics. They had fielded top drivers like Curtis Turner, Marvin Panch, Fireball Roberts, Parnelli Jones, Tiny Lund, Junior Johnson, Speedy Thompson, and

Fred Lorenzen. Leonard Wood had designed techniques to lessen the car's time spent on pit road, essentially creating what we now know as the pit stop. While the other teams looked like the Keystone Kops during a pit stop, the Wood Brothers team performed their stops with the precision of a fine watch, each member of the crew performing specific duties in harmony with the rest. They were the first to realize that races could be won or lost in the pits.

It was so hot in the car that day that each time the car would pit, they would pour cold water on Cale's feet. The soles of his shoes were melting and sticking to the floorboard.

Under the tutelage of the Wood brothers, Cale learned to go faster by slowing down a little. Keeping the race car slightly below maximum output allowed it to last longer, and Cale began to realize that one of the main ingredients to a race win was to finish. Communication between Cale and the Wood brothers continued to improve. Cale had never been too mechanical in nature, but Glen and Leonard could decipher Cale's description of how the car was handling and translate it to the suspension setup of the car almost exactly to his liking. No other team before had understood him so well.

The Southern 500 in Darlington served as Cale's coming-home party, and it felt good to be back behind the wheel of a stock car again. It was as comfortable as sleeping in his own bed. It was so hot in the car that day that each time the car would pit, they would pour cold water on Cale's feet. The soles of his shoes were melting and sticking to the floorboard. He led for 33 laps and finished 11th. In four of the last five races of the 1966 season, Cale started in the top 10. Only having run 14 races the entire season, he had eclipsed his prior year's earnings, winning more than $28,000.

The Wood Brothers team started the 1967 season with a bang. Cale had reached the point that any time he lined up on the starting line, he didn't just know he could win, he expected to win. The #21 Ford qualified in the top 10 every week, until Cale finally put the car on the pole at Atlanta. It was his first pole in the Grand National series, and it came at a superspeedway. That weekend, all the stars must have been aligned, for it was also Cale's first superspeedway victory. He had battled with the lap-down car of Mario Andretti for several laps at the end of the race until he was finally able to pull around him to take the checkered flag. That weekend alone paid him more than $20,000, split 50/50 with the Wood Brothers, the customary arrangement. He took his share of the winnings, invested in a dry cleaning business in Hartsville, and bought another 500 acres of land.

Cale decided again that he would like to run at Indy, but this time he kept his NASCAR ride arrangement intact. This led to a particularly busy Memorial

Day weekend for Cale, as he contested Indy on Friday, flew to Charlotte, and ran the 600-miler there on Sunday. He was able to pull out a 17th place finish in Indy, but only after tangling with Lee Roy Yarbrough, who was also running both events, and Lloyd Ruby. The collision sent Yarbrough and Ruby into the wall, ending their day on the track. After a quick flight to Charlotte, Cale jumped in the stock car and qualified it on the pole, setting a new track record in the process. His race ended early when the engine gave up after only 58 laps. All in all, though, it had been a successful racing weekend.

Each race yielded more of the same, with every qualifying effort a top 10 and every finish in the top 10 unless the race was cut short by mechanical problems or a crash. Cale was in Daytona on July 4 to run the Firecracker 400. He had led this event two years earlier, but the gremlins showed up and took the race from him. He hoped this year would yield better results. His Ford was running strong, as usual, and he started the race from the outside of the front row. There was a long stretch of the race without any caution flags for an opportunity to pit without losing time and track position. Cale began preserving fuel in search of a yellow, but it never came. He stayed on the track one lap too long and, as the car rounded Turn 1, he felt it sputter. He was out of fuel. He nursed the car back around the track and down pit road for service, but his team was unaware of the situation and wasn't ready for him to come in. It was obvious to Cale that they were not prepared for him, so he passed his pit box and ran straight to Junior Johnson's (now a car owner for Lee Roy Yarbrough) pit, where Junior had noticed Cale's plight. Junior's pit crew flew into action, fueling Cale and sending him back out on the track. Of course, it was against the rules for another crew to perform the service, but NASCAR had not yet hardened its stance on some of the rules and let it pass without comment. When they went to Junior's team for explanation, Junior just told them that he had not realized that it was not their driver they had fueled up. In retrospect, this incident defined the familiar atmosphere between the NASCAR drivers. Cale went on to win the race, his first Daytona victory.

Each year was bringing with it new successes, and 1967 was the best yet. Cale had qualified on the pole four times, won two races, and took home more than $57,000 in prize money. Not bad for a season in which he had only contested 17 of 49 events, finishing 20th in points. Nine of those 17 starts had ended early, so it was easy to see that if Cale was in the field, he was going to be up front.

For 1968, the Wood Brothers fielded the red and white #21 Mercury with Cale aboard for what turned out to be their best year together. Daytona, at the start of the season, gave a preview of what was to come, with Cale's Mercury being the class of the field of 50 contestants. The qualifying races were rained out, but when they all went out for fast-lap qualifying, the #21 sat on the pole at a record-breaking 189+ mph. Cale led the field around the big oval for the first 20 or 30 laps, then the ignition began to cut out partway around the track and he had to hit the pits. The efficient pit crew showed their superiority by changing the ignition box and putting Cale back on the track only three laps down. It was Cale at his very best as he put the Mercury on the perfect line lap after lap, passing all others at will while making like a freight train back to the front of the field. Lee Roy Yarbrough had been leading the field while Cale was making his way back through. Cale caught up on Lap 89, leading to a duel that would last until Lap 200, when the checkered flag fell with Cale at the point. The race had been a spectator's dream, with the two swapping the lead time after time. Lee Roy was driving another Mercury for Junior Johnson, who had traded the cockpit for the owner's seat at the track. The win was worth more than $47,000, certainly a jump-start to a successful season. The pit work had certainly played a huge part in

It was Cale at his very best as he put the Mercury on the perfect line lap after lap, passing all others at will while making like a freight train back to the front of the field.

the win, and from that race forward, NASCAR became more of a team sport, as the crew often held the key to victory.

The other teams took notice of the importance of the time lost on pit road, and each took its cues from the Wood Brothers in forming their own ballet there. Within the next couple of years, all the teams could perform a routine pit stop involving tires and fuel in about 18 seconds. The Wood Brothers still led the pack when other work was needed, with each team member knowing exactly what his task was even before the car turned onto pit road.

The performance at Daytona propelled Cale to the top of the racing charts for the first time. He was being compared to all the great drivers he had always admired. His name would be mentioned alongside Richard Petty, David Pearson, and the rest, not as one of their competitors, but as an equal, and sometimes even better. He savored being the number one Grand National driver even more because his good friend Lee Roy was right behind him in second. Their relationship had grown tighter as time passed, and Cale always wanted the best for him. They were being touted in the newspapers as overnight successes. "Overnight" must have lasted about 10 years, as well as Cale could figure.

Wins would follow at Atlanta, Martinsville, Daytona, Darlington, and Jefferson. The Darlington win was particularly sweet, with Cale leading 169 of the 364 laps. After starting on the outside of the front row, he jumped into the lead. Paul Goldsmith, in a Dodge, was running strong, applying consistent pressure. Cale was leading David Pearson by a few seconds late in the race when the drivers pitted for the last time. The pit stop was typical for the Wood Brothers, and Cale was back on the racing surface in no time flat. Cale towed the field lap after lap, keeping a watchful eye on Pearson behind him. The line that was working best for Cale involved a slight brush with the fourth-turn wall. The car was running perfectly, but Cale began hearing noises that he hadn't heard before. Each time he would come out of Turn 4, the noise would get louder and louder. He kept watch on his gauges, and all seemed well, but how could that be so with all the noise? The laps wound down, and as Cale rounded Turn 4 for the last time, the rear end wobbled. He gathered it in, dashed for the start/finish line, and took the checkered flag. The Darlington track was due to be improved and slightly reconfigured for the upcoming season, so this was Cale's last chance to win at the original Darlington layout.

His hometown following had always been supportive, and to win at his "home" track was particularly gratifying. When the season ended, Cale had sat on the pole four times, won six races, finished in the top five 12 times, and led 1,065 laps. Again, he had not been able to finish nine of the 21 races started.

Cale had won more than $138,000 in purse money, $5,000 more than David Pearson, who had ran 48 races to finish in the points lead and second on the money list. He was voted Driver of the Year and was now a fan favorite. He had returned home after his first Daytona win to a hero's welcome, complete with the red carpet, high school marching band, parade, and confetti. The years of hard work, disappointment, crashes, and engine failures melted away, and tears filled his eyes. The small-town environment that had nurtured his growth meant more to him now than it ever had. The next Monday he made arrangements with the school in Timmonsville to set up a program to make sure that the students who could not afford school lunch would be fed, and the bill sent to him each month. It was something Cale had always promised himself he would do if he could ever afford it.

> **The years of hard work, disappointment, crashes, and engine failures melted away, and tears filled his eyes. The small-town environment that had nurtured his growth meant more to him now than it ever had.**

Another event of 1968 helped shape the course of Cale's life. The June race at Rockingham had been rained out. Cale joined other drivers in the drivers' lounge to discuss the situation and determine his plans for the balance of the weekend. Lee Roy had been keeping track of the weather, and it looked as if the storm was tracking toward the northeast, away from the Florence area. Cale made the decision to fly back home for the evening, so he loaded Betty Jo and Julie into his Bonanza. It was still raining, but it didn't seem bad enough to alter their plans. As the plane climbed to 5,000 feet, Cale began to look for the ceiling of the storm but could only see more of the thick, dense moisture. The rain increased in force and volume until it had obscured what little vision the clouds were kind enough to allow. Cale could not see the prop directly in front of him, his vision was so limited. He glanced over at his bride and daughter, and, feeling his responsibility for their safety, resolved right then and there to land the plane safely. If only he had not spent the hour or so talking racing with the boys in the lounge before leaving, he might have been able to take off ahead of this storm. He climbed higher, trying to break out of the clouds, but was only greeted by the flashes of lightning that would strobe them. He leveled out at about 13,000 feet, with the turbulence becoming more intense. The Bonanza was being tossed around in the air like an oak leaf in a fall breeze. Knowing he was headed for the Great Pee Dee River Swamp, Cale banked and turned the plane around. If he landed in the swamp, they might never be found. The rain seemed to get even worse, and the engine began to sputter. Cale suspected it was being drowned out, and knew they were in real trouble. He cut back on the throttle in a futile attempt to get the engine firing properly, but after a few minutes of worsening sputter, the engine retired completely, leaving the craft solely at the mercy of God and the winds.

Through it all, little was being said in the cockpit of the plane. Betty Jo and Julie sat wide-eyed as the situation worsened. They watched as Cale tried to maintain some sort of control, working the controls until sweat broke out on his forehead. Betty Jo laid her hand on Cale's arm, and he could feel the faith she had in him through the gentle physical contact. The rain was still pounding as hard as ever, and the wind sent the plane in all directions, straight up until it stalled, then straight down. No matter how Cale moved the controls, the plane refused to respond. They were losing precious altitude, but the gauges were frozen, so Cale had no idea how far from the ground he might be. Lightning lit up the sky regularly, and during one instance of brightness, he broke through the clouds just above a dirt road. Nothing elaborate, it

> No matter how Cale moved the controls, the plane refused to respond. They were losing precious altitude, but the gauges were frozen, so Cale had no idea how far from the ground he might be.

had been cut through the pines by loggers, but they had cut the road long and straight. Fresh from the storm, it might as well have been Kennedy Airport to Cale, who was able to perform a dead-stick landing with no more commotion than the water and mud flying by as they taxied to a stop aided by the deep muck. Still, it was quiet in the plane, and they all collected themselves and gave thanks to God for the safe landing. Not once was it mentioned that they might crash. So strong was Cale's resolve, he probably never even considered anything but a happy ending.

Now all they needed was a ride home, so Cale left the girls to find help. He knew there would be no houses on the logging road, so he chose a direction and began his hike. After several miles, he turned around and returned to the plane. It was approaching nightfall, so they decided to spend the night in the plane. Cale would head in the other direction in the morning. They pulled some blankets from the rear of the plane and made themselves as comfortable as possible. They were awakened shortly after dawn by a pounding on the plane door. Three Marines were patrolling the area in a Jeep when they had come across the plane sitting in the middle of the road. The pines they had landed in covered 10 square miles, and they had landed square in the middle. The Marines took the family to the nearest country store. James Garner and Dickie

Smothers were the only people Cale could remember who were staying overnight in Rockingham, so he called and had them come to pick up the three of them and take them home.

Cale knew a fellow in Pinehurst with whom he arranged the retrieval of the plane. After the weather passed, the road dried enough that the Bonanza could be dug out. A crop duster was hired to fly the plane out. When Cale saw the plane, all the paint had been erased from the wings, leaving them trimmed only in shiny aluminum. The plane was put on the market and was replaced by a twin-engined craft.

He could have, at any time, accepted that danger might take him, but he was determined that, if he had anything to do with it, danger would not take his family from him.

With all the incredible moments Cale had previously experienced, that plane ride affected him differently than any of the rest. He had found himself facing peril many times, and enjoyed the adrenaline rush that automatically accompanies imminent danger, but the incident in the plane had also involved his family. Cale had always looked danger straight in the eyes, developing a sense of understanding how to conquer the moment of fear that defines the very word. He could have, at any time, accepted that danger might take him, but he was determined that, if he had anything to do with it, danger would not take his family from him. He never again took the family along in the airplane after that flight from Rockingham.

Cale and the Wood Brothers partnered again for the 1969 season, with Cale contesting 19 of the 54 events. Only twice did Cale qualify the #21 red-and-white Mercury outside the top five spots, and that was an 11th at both Riverside and Rockingham. Overall, he took six poles, resulting in wins at Atlanta and Michigan. He had only completed eight of the 19 events, but still earned purse money of more than $75,000 with wins at Atlanta and Michigan. It was a year that saw David Pearson unleash his power on the track, winning the points race for the championship by a respectable margin over Richard Petty.

The 1969 season had been successful for Cale, but had treated his good friend Lee Roy even better. Lee Roy ran his best season yet, winning seven times, and finishing in the top 10 21 times in the 30 races entered. Lee Roy's win total in Grand National mirrored Cale's 11, which seemed pretty appropriate since their careers and driving styles were so similar. They had both begun on the dirt tracks of South Carolina, graduated to Grand National around the same time, contested Indy together, and traveled so many miles and tracks together that many fans thought, perhaps, they were brothers or cousins. Their surnames were only one letter different from each other, so the mistake was understandable.

Lee Roy was testing tires at the Texas Motor Speedway in his #98 Junior Johnson Ford during the 1970 season when things went completely wrong on the track, sending him head-on into the wall at full speed. There had not been time to swing the car sideways to help absorb some of the impact from the crash, and he was hurt badly. Cale visited him in the hospital, and although his body looked just like Lee Roy, there was the strangest look on his face and in his eyes. He seemed detached, and his stare was distant. Cale left the visit wondering if Lee Roy had even recognized him.

Several weeks later, there was a race in Rockingham. Cale called Lee Roy to see if he wanted to share the plane ride, and they arranged for Cale to pick him up at the Columbia airport. When Cale arrived, Lee Roy looked physically sound, but there was still that distant look in his eyes. Cale was glad he was doing the flying. The race at Rockingham ended with Cale following Richard Petty across the finish line, and although Lee Roy had qualified 11th, he drove a very conservative race, finishing in the 29 position. It was a different Lee Roy than had been seen before.

On the return flight, the cockpit was quiet. Cale tried several times to engage in conversation, but Lee Roy would just nod his head to signal his reply. Cale saw him again the next week, but Lee Roy didn't seem to even remember going to the Rockingham track, and had no recollection of the race itself. He tried to bluff that he remembered, but Cale knew better by the way he answered.

Lee Roy was never the same, and his track performances were lackluster in comparison to his previous races. He finished the season with Junior, but early in the next season he was released from the team. Bill Seifert provided a ride, and Lee Roy showed up and ran, but his pole days and wins were all behind him now. Before the Firecracker 400 in Daytona, Jim Hunter had arranged to pick him up at the airport. They had been specific about the timing, but as Jim circled the rotunda, he didn't see Lee Roy anywhere. On his third rotation, he finally recognized his old friend. Lee Roy was unshaven, with a big beer belly that overhung his beltline. His hair had turned white, and he was ridiculously dressed in plaid slacks with a dirty old striped sport coat. As Jim pulled to the curb, Lee Roy asked if he was there for him. They made their way to the track, but Jim was never sure if his old friend even knew who he was.

A short time later, there was news that Lee Roy had tried to kill his mother and he was admitted to a mental institution. The drivers passed the hat, raising a substantial amount of money for his treatment. Junior visited him there, but came away empty-hearted, as Lee Roy not only couldn't remember who Junior was, he had also forgotten that he had ever driven a race car. It seemed such a shame, because for the 1969 season, he had been at the top of the heap, unanimously voted Driver of the Year, the only time that had ever happened.

Many from the racing community showed support for Lee Roy over the years he spent in the hospital. They visited him, but he never remembered any of his glory days. His condition worsened over time, and 14 years after the tragic crash, he passed away from a brain hemorrhage. Cale mourned the passing of such a great friend and comrade.

The new decade started with a big change in NASCAR. In 1972, R.J. Reynolds began to sponsor the entire Grand National series, and the name changed to the Winston Cup Series. The last year of the Wood Brothers/Yarborough partnership came in 1970, but neither knew it at the time. Together, they entered 19 of the 48 events, and, again, the red-and-white Mercury qualified in the top 10 for every race, save Talladega, where Cale was able to move up from his 21st starting position to finish the race fifth. He sat on the pole another five times. Daytona yielded another victory, as did Michigan and Rockingham. Another $117,000 went to the bank account from the purse money. Cale's reputation on the track bordered on superstar, with perhaps the only deterrent to full-blown stardom being that he ran so few races each year. If he had run in all 48 events, what would his totals and his celebrity have been like?

All the major manufacturers had, at some time or other, used racing as a platform to spotlight their products. "Win on Sunday, Sell on Monday" became a popular mantra in the business, based solely on actual results in the showrooms. NASCAR fans were very loyal to the car brand that carried their favorite driver around the track. Therefore, it caught the racing community by surprise when the Ford Motor Company's Ford Racing Division closed its doors on December 4, 1970. Ford had worked directly with several Grand National teams, supplying special parts and sharing technologies developed within their well-funded walls. Their cars had dominated Indy for quite some time. They had made the decision in the mid-1960s to win at LeMans against the formidable Ferrari team, and within just a few years crossed the finish line first, second, and third. The drag strips had been kind, as well, with special "lightweight" models available with big V8 engines for straight-line competition. All of the racing activities ceased in one cruel moment. It had seemed that Ford could win at will, so their departure from competition certainly represented a change of direction. With the Wood Brothers being direct beneficiaries of the factory effort, their pullout signaled the end of Cale's Ford ride for the 1971 season.

When Cale had lost his last ride, he had gone to Indy in '66 and '67. The plan had worked in his favor, and the gained exposure did nothing but enhance his career. Gene White was a tire dealer in

Atlanta, and now offered Cale a ride as the driver for his second team. Cale's old friend Lloyd Ruby piloted the first team's car, and welcomed him into the fold, offering help and advice without any resentment whatsoever. White fielded Mongoose chassis with turbocharged Ford engines, strong cars but not quite up to the standards being set by the Eagle, Brabham, McLaren, and Coyote teams.

Of the 88 cars vying for the 33 starting spots available, Lloyd qualified his car seventh, while Cale sat in the 14th position after running a lap speed of 170.156 mph. Peter Revson sat on the pole with a lap speed of 178.696 mph in the rocket built by McLaren. When race day arrived, attrition was the word for the day. Only 10 drivers finished the race. Cale finished 16th after being sidelined with 60 laps to go after a valve cover loosened, spilling all his oil. Lloyd started strong, running up front, but again the gremlins returned when he experienced gear problems on Lap 174. It seemed that every time Ruby led a race, his day would be cut short by the failure of a small part. Even though he left the race 26 laps early, it was still good enough for an 11th-place finish.

Cale only ran four races in Winston Cup for 1971, driving a Plymouth for Ray Fox in Daytona, twice, and Atlanta. In Charlotte, he drove a Mercury for James Mason. The best he could muster was a seventh-place finish in Atlanta. It turned out to be an "also-ran"-type season for the veteran.

He drove again in Indy for Gene White in 1972, starting at the rear of the field and working his way up to a 10th-place finish. He probably would have finished much better had he not run out of gas about halfway through the race. He lost two laps in the process, too great a margin to recoup in an ill-handling car. Cale had never gotten the knack of reading the open-wheelers like he could a stock car, so he couldn't give his crew much opportunity to adjust the car to provide better performance. All he could do was hang on and drive the car that was beneath him.

He had not immediately risen through the ranks in Indy cars, and was feeling dissatisfied with the results.

Cale only drove in five Winston Cup races during the '72 season. Ray Fox hired him to drive the #3 Plymouth in Daytona, where he finished sixth. He was in James Hylton's #98 Mercury when he crossed the finish line in fifth for the Yankee 400 in Michigan. Hoss Ellington provided the #28 Chevrolet in Charlotte, Rockingham, and Texas, yielding another sixth place finish at the Rock and a ninth in Texas.

Two seasons away from regular action in the Winston Cup series tended to make Cale a little homesick for the cars he had raced for so long. He had not immediately risen through the ranks in Indy cars, and was feeling dissatisfied with the results. He had become accustomed to the winning atmosphere he had left behind, so he began to long for a good stock-car ride. He knew it wouldn't be in a Ford, as they had truly left racing, concentrating on meeting government mandates for safety and fuel efficiency. His break came when Bobby Allison decided he was going to field his own car, leaving Junior Johnson's Chevrolet without a driver. Junior offered Cale the ride, which he was quick to accept. Junior was already a NASCAR legend, with his racing history dating back to the earliest days. He had learned to drive on the back roads as a moonshine hauler, tangling with the law and building a reputation—perhaps unfounded—as a renegade. In actuality, Junior was a kind, likeable man who was always honest in his dealings. He had just been a product of his upbringing and environment— he hailed from the mountain areas where making white liquor was considered a birthright. Hauling the illicit goods was just another way to make a living, even if it meant driving at full speed through the back roads of Carolina and Virginia with the lights out so as not to attract the attention of federal agents. This wild kind of driving served as excellent training for the fledgling NASCAR and their Strictly Stock series.

Several other moonshine haulers joined the ranks of the racers, making for some interesting stories that might seem as if they were taken from Hollywood movies, even though there was more truth in those stories than fiction. Bob Flock, Buddy Shuman, and Curtis Turner were some of the others who got into racing as a more legitimate way of earning their pay. Sometimes the police would show up at a track specifically to catch these moonshine haulers, making for some interesting circumstances. Once, at Lakewood, near Atlanta, police literally chased Bob Flock around the track until he made a quick exit through an open back gate. The race car left the track followed by a handful of police cars with sirens wailing as they sped through the downtown streets of Atlanta. The chase ended when Flock ran low on fuel and surrendered to the authorities.

Junior showed exceptional talent from his first venture on the track. He caught the attention of Bill France, who was fighting to make his racing series grow. Bill approached Junior after a good run and told him, "Junior, you're doing pretty good out there. In fact, you're doing so well that we expect you to run all 30 races next year." He wanted Junior in the field.

Junior considered what France had said, then answered, "Naw, Bill, I'm only going to run a few races to see if I like it or not."

Bill pleaded, "But you're committed, Junior."

"Naw, Bill, what I am is *involved*."

"You're committed, Junior." This time it sounded more like he meant it.

After a minute, Junior looked at Bill and said, "Bill, you've got your words all wrong. Now listen, if you sit down to breakfast tomorrow to bacon and eggs, the chicken is involved. The pig is committed."

Junior ended up running the races he wanted to.

NASCAR had done a lot of growing since those earliest days. Now they were fielding what looked like showroom cars in style but were actually purpose-built machines in street clothes. Less of the races were being contested on the short dirt tracks, as new speedways were built. Larger crowds at the races led to greater opportunities for sponsors to cash in on the rush. Larger corporations were beginning to explore the value of race and driver sponsorships, pouring money into the coffers. Sometimes it was as if the sponsors were racing away from the track to outspend their competitors, and then again on the track, letting their driver do the racing for them. Cars were being painted in brighter colors to attract the crowd's attention, and corporate and secondary sponsorship logos adorned their flanks. It was a new day in stock-car racing, but an allegiance with Junior created a bridge to the past for Cale. He had joined the NASCAR ranks early enough to have experienced some of the mischief created by the characters on the track, but clearly he fit into the mold being cast by these new sponsors. These sponsors wanted respectability from their drivers and demanded certain behavioral standards that reflected their corporate values.

Landing the ride with Junior changed Cale's life in several ways. The 1973 season would be the first year Cale would run in all the scheduled events, 28 in total. His travel schedule exploded, and his time at home was cut to a fraction of what he was used to. The skills he had developed over the years would be sharpened, then honed to a razor's edge, by the week-to-week grind that makes up the NASCAR season. Junior pushed Cale to preserve equipment for the end of the race, just like the Wood Brothers had tried to do. Perhaps it was Cale's level of maturity that allowed him to accept the challenge from Junior as being crucial to a successful season. It wasn't uncommon for Cale to take himself out of a race by pushing a car at or over its perceived limits lap after lap until it expired. Richard Petty and David Pearson had a sly driving style, running their machines just as hard as necessary to produce the best finish. Often they wouldn't show their full potential in a race until the last series of laps, when they would stave off the competition in a mad dash for the checkered flag. It was doubtful that Cale would ever be as passive as that. He had always charged hard from start to finish, with each lap seeming to be the most important. Junior taught Cale to give the final lap more respect than the others, and the results were immediate and substantial.

> **Junior taught Cale to give the final lap more respect than the others, and the results were immediate and substantial.**

Junior's Chevrolet was as good as any car on the track, and Herb Nab built engines that not only pumped out plenty of horsepower but stayed together as well. Stable sponsorship from Richard Howard and his Kar Kare company kept the team's concentration on racing. Each week, at each track, they arrived ready to win. Cale qualified 27 of the 28 races in the top 10, including five poles. Mechanical woes became less frequent, but there were the unavoidable crashes that happen all too frequently. The #11 Kar Kare Chevrolet finished 20 of the races, 19 of them in the top 10, and 16 of those in the top five. He had won four races, Bristol twice, Darlington, and Charlotte. The Bristol win is still in the record books. It was the only time a driver led all of the 500 laps. It also still stands as the

He was running so much faster than the rest of the field that Bud Moore, the television commentator, made the comment that Cale had better watch out or he would lap his own shadow.

most laps led in any race. Cale started from the pole, rocketed away from the field, and never looked back. He had lapped the field twice by the last lap. He was running so much faster than the rest of the field that Bud Moore, the television commentator, remarked that Cale had better watch out or he would lap his own shadow. He displayed the same dominance at Nashville, leading all but four of the 420 laps, again winning by two laps. Only Benny Parsons, the cautious one, ended the year with more championship points than Cale. Cale's wallet was the fattest at the end of the season, having earned more than $267,000.

Nineteen seventy-four began as an extension of the previous season. Cale ran in all 30 races, qualifying in the top 10 in all of them. He finished 23 times, with 22 top 10s and 21 top fives, including 10 wins. As good as his year had been, Richard Petty had been better, winning the points championship comfortably, putting more than $432,000 in the bank. Cale took home more than $363,000, finishing second in the championship standings for another season. Midway through the season, there had been a sponsorship change for Cale, and now he wore the Carling uniform. In addition to the money he had earned, he had also earned the kind of respect reserved for only the best drivers in the business. The sign as you entered his hometown of Timmonsville now read: Timmonsville, SC, Home of Cale Yarborough, NASCAR Champion. All the fuss did little to change Cale, who was still the old farmer he'd always been. He still went hunting and fishing with his buddies and wore the same old overalls with the holes and missing hardware he had always worn.

Carling pulled its sponsorship after the '74 season, so Junior and Cale began the season hunting for a new backer. They landed Holly Farms Chicken as a sponsor for their bid at Darlington, and the combination worked out for the rest of the season and further. Nineteen seventy-five turned out to be a hard-luck season, as they failed to finish in 14 races. The first run at Talladega ended early when the speeds blew Cale's windshield into his lap, ending his day after only 19 laps. It was just that type of year. They still salvaged a respectable showing, with three victories and winnings totaling almost $200,000. It had been a year of tragedy for Cale, though, as he lost good friend Tiny Lund at their second Talladega run. He and Tiny were to fly home together after the race to Tiny's fishing camp in Cross, South Carolina, but it never came to pass.

Tiny found himself sideways during the race, sending him into the outer wall. He bounced off the wall back across the track, and was hit square in the driver's door by almost two tons of car running 200 mph. When Cale passed on the first caution lap, he could see Tiny slumped over the wheel, and he knew that to survive such a hit would be almost impossible. He looked away each lap he passed until they had removed Tiny's lifeless body from the car. Tiny had always been there, his traveling partner and friend. He remembered all the nights they had slept in the car at the different tracks, all the fun they had shared. The green flag fell again, with Cale able to store all his thoughts of Tiny in the back of his mind, but he couldn't suppress them altogether. Tiny had been the closest to him of all the drivers.

Cale qualified for his first race in the International Race of Champions series in '75. The IROC series was designed to find the best driver in the world each year. Drivers from different racing series worldwide qualify for one of the 12 spots available. All the drivers drove identically prepared Camaros in four events—Michigan, two at Riverside, and the finale at Daytona. Cale finished out the year in third, behind Bobby Unser and A.J. Foyt.

He had finally become the elite driver he had always imagined.

The '76 season began a sensational run for the Holly Farms team. Who knew that they were beginning a run that would still stand in the record books more than 30 years later? They contested all 30 events, fighting a fierce battle with Richard Petty for the points lead. In the next to last race at Atlanta, Petty suffered engine problems, finishing down in the field and giving Cale an insurmountable lead. Nine wins and 23 top 10s—22 of them top fives—earned Cale his first Winston Cup championship and over $453,000 in winnings. Of the 10,010 laps that constituted the season, he had led 3,791 of them. He won four races in a row toward the end of the season. Whether at a short track or superspeedway, he was always making a bid for the victory. He had even won on the road course at Riverside twice in '74 and finished second in '76. He had finally become the elite driver he had always imagined. He had joined the ranks of Petty, Pearson, and Allison, and his résumé of records began to grow. He had become famous, having received a stamp of approval from even the harshest critics.

Beginning the 1977 season as the standing champion brings with it added media interest and other distractions that can interfere with a driver's concentration on racing. Not so with Cale. He relished the added attention, as always. He seemed at home in front of the camera or with a microphone in his face. It did nothing to divert his focus—in fact, it might have even intensified it. In what was a phenomenal year, the gold-and-white #11 Holly Farms Chevrolet ran all 30 races, qualifying in the top 10, including three poles, in all of them. Cale added another nine victories among his 27 top 10 finishes, 25 of which were top fives. Perhaps the most impressive statistic of the year was a perfect finish ratio, with only 120 laps not run in the whole season. No other driver has finished every race in a single season. He had led another 3,219 of the 9,867 lap season, winning more than $561,000, eclipsing second place Richard Petty by more than $150,000. Benny Parsons finished the season third in points, and a young Darrell Waltrip ended up fourth, his first top-five season. Junior had somehow put all of the puzzle together. Only Joe Weatherly, David Pearson, and Richard Petty had ever won two championships in a row, placing Cale in the record books again.

Cale qualified for the IROC series this year as well. At the third race at Riverside, he tamed the road course with his Camaro, leading every lap. At Daytona, five drivers shared the lead between them, Cale being one of them. He was the last driver to lead, pulling ahead on the final lap to take the checkered flag. His dismal finishes in the first two races gave the points lead to A.J. Foyt for his second championship in a row.

The Junior Johnson racing team made the change to Oldsmobile for the 1978 season, with First National City Travelers Checks as the sponsor. Cale just kept on driving like the champion he had become. Running away with the championship looked like it might become a habit. He started the season with a win on the road track at Riverside and found victory lane nine more times throughout the 30 races. His qualifying remained consistently top 10, including eight more starts from the pole. He led another 3,587 laps, letting the field see his taillights more often than his grille. There were only two races shortened by mechanical failures. In the end, it all added up to Cale's most dominant season, winning the championship by his largest margin. He took home a record-breaking $623,506. He had become the first driver ever to win three championships in a row. Richard Petty might have earned the nickname "the King," but for now, Cale was sitting firmly on the throne. He was at the pinnacle of his career. Through the three championship seasons, Cale had won 28 of 90 races.

The 1979 season began with a bang. Literally! The Oldsmobile now wore the Busch logo on its hood, finishing third in Riverside, then the team trekked back across the country for the big Daytona race. CBS broadcast the race live on television, a first for NASCAR. Their races had generally been broadcast in clips for sports exclusives. The nationwide exposure immediately expanded NASCAR's boundaries, attracting a throng of new fans. The networks might have held out because of the length of the events, thinking that it would be difficult to keep the audience's attention. If that was the case, the '79 Daytona 500 would change their minds. It had rained, and the track had to be dried off before the start of the race. Bobby and Donnie Allison came together between Turns 1 and 2 right in front of Cale, who had to spin into the muddy infield to avoid a crash. His car was bogged in the mud, requiring a wrecker to get it back to the track. It was two long laps later when he rejoined the group. He drove the Olds with abandon, making up his laps and catching Donnie, who had made it to the front. At that point, Cale fell into the draft of the Allison machine and held his position. He knew he had some reserve horses under the hood, so he made his plan for a pass through Turn 4 and a drag race to the finish that he could not lose. Coming out of

Turn 2, Cale saw that the lapped car of Bobby Allison was positioning itself to allow Bobby to help Donnie win the race by blocking for him. It was now or never, so Cale pulled below Donnie at the entrance to the rear straightaway. Donnie moved his car closer toward the inside, forcing Cale down onto the apron, then across the wet grass. At 200 mph, he skimmed the surface of the slick grass, steering right to get back to the track. The two cars came together again, this time pushing the cars across the track. One more time they came together, but this time Cale's wheels were aimed toward the Allison machine. He had had enough, and both cars careened off the outside retaining wall, sliding into the infield. Richard Petty had been holding the third position several seconds behind Cale before the crash and cruised to an easy victory. The real action was in the infield, though. Usually a gentleman, Cale had become enraged with the incident. Bobby had pulled his car onto the grass and was running back to help his brother. Cale leapt from his bruised Oldsmobile, ran over to Bobby, and decked him. Then he ran over to Donnie, giving him a knuckle sandwich. It was all caught on camera for the nation to see. Daytona had been the scene of many exciting finishes, but this one was the most exciting ever, and

Cale leapt from his bruised Oldsmobile, ran over to Bobby, and decked him.

it could not have happened at a better time for NASCAR, whose popularity soared, marking the beginning of a new era.

National exposure brought new opportunities for marketing, reflected in the new sponsorships attracted to the sport. Television exposure expanded the audience from the 100,000 or so at the track to millions over the airways. The promotion of T-shirts, caps, and other memorabilia began to capture millions of dollars in revenue, essentially starting a new industry that eclipsed $1 billion in sales by 1998. Of course, costs to race changed just as much. In 1949, a stock car could be fielded for the price of the car, as little as a thousand dollars. The price of a good car had risen to over $100,000 by the late '80s, and teams would generally have a stable of cars, some built specifically for short tracks, some for the speedways. Travel expenses were huge, transporting the entire team and equipment the length of the country twice in a season. The attraction of these major corporate sponsors was not just a boon to the sport, it was a necessity. Purses had grown exponentially as well, attested to by Cale's earnings year to year. But even the substantial purse money didn't provide enough fuel to keep the fire burning all by itself. It took the financial support of a pretty good-sized company to remain competitive. Junior and Cale were quite fortunate to be able to attract a sponsor as respected as Busch.

Richard Petty won his seventh and last championship in 1979, edging out Darrell Waltrip by the narrowest of margins. Cale finished the season fourth in points behind Bobby Allison. He had won another four races, qualified in the top 10 for all but two races, and led another 1,323 laps on his way to over $440,000 in earnings. The next season Cale flexed his muscles again. He started 20 of the 31 races from the front row. Of his 22 top 10s, six were victories. It was almost enough for another championship. A late-season charge pulled the margin tighter, but he fell 19 points short of Dale Earnhardt to finish second. Winning more than $567,000 in prize monies, his total winnings with Junior had exceeded $3 million.

Cale and Junior had raced together for eight successful years, and it looked as if the relationship could continue indefinitely. Mountain Dew was entertaining sponsorship for Junior's team for the 1981 season. Cale was at home and had just dressed for the trip to the airport to go to the meeting when he came across his daughter, B.J., and some of her friends sitting on the back steps.

"Why are you just sitting around? Why aren't you out riding your bike or something?" he asked the girls.

"My bike is broken, Daddy."

"Well, why didn't you tell me about it?" Cale inquired.

"I did, Daddy, I told you three times," B.J. replied.

"You mean to tell me that you told me three times that your bike was broken, and I didn't do anything about it?" Cale wasn't enjoying this feeling.

"That's right," the girls answered as a group.

"You all wait right there," he told the girls as he headed back inside the house.

He picked up the telephone and called the Mountain Dew people. He explained that he had a situation at home that needed his attention and that he would not be able to make the meeting.

He threw on his old jeans and a work shirt and spent the next two days repairing all the girls' bikes.

As Cale surveyed the situation as it had been revealed to him by his youngest daughter, he realized that all the traveling had kept him from home more than he had ever planned. He looked at his life as it was and felt that he had enough money for the rest of his life. He had done quite well and had not squandered his earnings but put them to work for him. He had made sound investments—a Honda/Mazda dealership in Florence, several dry-cleaning locations, a Goodyear tire distributorship (with partner Billy Atkinson), some rental property, and several parcels of farmland. He had paid a price for his good fortune in the time and attention he had not been able to give those who were most important to him. Maybe it had been worth it all, but now he felt it was time to give to his family. Immediate resolve was made to cut his racing involvement in half.

Cale hated to give up his ride with Junior. They had really enjoyed their relationship and the success it had brought them, but Cale knew what he had to do. He went to Junior and explained how he wanted to cut back on his racing schedule and why. Junior completely understood, although he hated to lose Cale as much as Cale hated to leave. Junior was committed to the Mountain Dew folks to run every race in the '81 season, and there was no way to fit the two plans together.

Junior was able to woo Darrell Waltrip into his fold, beginning yet another successful run. Cale looked around until he hooked up with M.C. Anderson to run the superspeedways. He would now run just half of the Winston Cup races.

CHAPTER 6

The Car Owner

Part-time driving fit Cale like an old favorite tennis shoe. He could still feed his need for speed, and he could do it without sacrificing so much of his family time. It didn't slow him down on or off the track. His farm and businesses benefited from his added attention. He had built a beautiful brick home on a piece of property he had always wanted. Betty Jo and the girls became more a part of him, a part that he would never again be without. Life was about as good as it could get for the whole Yarborough family.

M.C. Anderson had been fielding Winston Cup cars since 1976, with drivers that included Buddy Baker and Benny Parsons. Benny had won five times in the '79 and '80 seasons, and had finished fifth and third in the points, running the entire schedule. M.C. was of a like mind as Cale in wanting to scale back to about half the races. The 1980 season had given up three victories on speedways, and the speedways were where Cale wanted to drive. Valvoline agreed to sponsor the program, so the team set out to build the best

Buicks they could build. They chose their schedule around the one-and-a-half mile and longer speedways, so they were able to concentrate on setups and aerodynamic tuning to fit. Cale took the #27 Valvoline Buick into the top 10 in 10 of the 18 contests. Seven races ended early, so if he finished, he finished strong. With wins at Atlanta and Daytona, he earned purses totaling over $150,000.

Rockingham, Michigan, and Darlington were winning tracks for Cale in the '82 season. The Valvoline team started 16 races, finishing only half of them. All eight of the full-race finishes were in the top five. It was a year that saw Darrell Waltrip win the Winston Cup with a slim points edge over Bobby Allison. Cale had his mechanical woes, but he still managed to pocket more than $231,000 in prize money. Anderson decided to fold the team after the season, so once again Cale looked around for a ride. It sure was easier to find a ride as a champion than it had back in the old dirt track days. The equipment was better, too. He struck a deal with Harry Ranier to drive the #28 Hardee's Chevrolet.

It still didn't matter what brand of car or which owner Cale teamed up with. He always seemed to be that one added ingredient that led to success. Their very first race together was the Daytona 500. Cale went out for his qualifying laps. On his first lap, he scored a track record 200.503 mph. On the second lap, he flipped the car at over 200 mph, destroying the car and erasing the record time because he didn't finish the effort. It was still the first time a Winston Cup car had achieved a 200+ mph run. Ranier pulled out the backup car, a Pontiac, with Cale starting back in the pack in 28th. Right foot planted on the floor and a firm handle on the wheel, Cale charged up through the field, displaying his many years of winning experience. Patience was now available when needed. As Cale would come up on the slower traffic, he had learned to assess the situation. He knew most of these drivers' styles and habits, would choose the appropriate action, make his move around them, then move forward to the next victim. One by one, he picked them off until there were no more. The checkered flag fell across the hood of Cale's car in Dayton again, and it was off to the races for Yarborough and the Ranier team.

The checkered flag fell across the hood of Cale's car in Dayton again, and it was off to the races for Yarborough and the Ranier team.

Bobby Allison and Darrell Waltrip fought another close battle for the Cup championship in 1983, with Allison leading Waltrip by about the same margin he had lost to Waltrip the year before. Bill Elliott, Richard Petty, and Terry Labonte completed the top five. Cale only ran 16 races, again only finishing in eight. All eight finishes were top 10 again, with four of them wins—Daytona, Atlanta, and both races at Michigan. He brought home $265,000 in winnings as a result of his continued winning ways.

The Daytona 500 had always been one of Cale's favorite races. He had won it three times, and, if his equipment could hold out, he could make it run up front. The #28 Hardee's Chevrolet sat on

Cale announced his retirement from racing at the end of the 1988 season.

the pole again in '84 and led 89 of the 200 laps. Darrell Waltrip was leading Cale and Dale Earnhardt until the white flag lap, when Cale made his move, pulling Earnhardt in his draft. It was the #28 that crossed the line eight car lengths ahead of the field. Petty had been the last to score two Daytona 500 victories in a row in '73 and '74. Qualifying had always been a special talent for Cale, and again in '84 he was able to take the Chevy to the pole four times. He dominated the race in Charlotte, leading 132 laps, before the engine expired for a disappointed ending of the day. Talladega and Pocono fell victim to his onslaught, and were added to the win column. More than $403,000 in winnings made it the most profitable season he had enjoyed since cutting back his schedule.

Engine troubles plagued the team in 1985 as they made the move from Chevrolet to Ford. They only completed seven of the 16 races they entered.

Cale continued to show that he was sharp as ever, as all seven races completed were top 10 finishes. Among those were wins at Talladega and Charlotte, avenging the previous year's DNF. The Charlotte win was number 83, and was to be his last. Nineteen eighty-six was a continuation of the mechanical woes, as he could only finish in six of the 16 races he entered. He finished the year with five top 10s. Cale was accustomed to more success than he was having, and decided it was time for another change, but this time the change would lead in a new direction.

Cale was accustomed to more success than he was having, and decided it was time for another change, but this time the change would lead in a new direction.

Cale bought the team from Ranier, and left Ford for Oldsmobile. He ran the '87 season as an owner/driver in 16 races. Keeping the Hardee's sponsorship but changing the car number to #29, Cale could only muster four top 10s. The combined duties of owner and driver demanded more of his time and effort, so for the 1988 season, he split driving duties with Dale Jarrett. Dale had one top 10 finish in his 19 starts. Cale managed two ninth place finishes from his 10 times behind the wheel.

Cale announced his retirement from racing at the end of the 1988 season.

Dale Jarrett became the full-time driver for 1989 in the #29 Pontiac, running in 29 races with five top 10 finishes, two of them in the top five. Hardee's pulled their sponsorship after the end of the season, replaced by Phillips 66/TropArtic.

Dick Trickle took over the driving responsibilities for the 1990 season, piloting the #66 Pontiac to four top 10s, two of them top fives. He enjoyed sitting on the pole the only time in his career in Dover, and earned more than $350,000 in prize monies. He began the '91 season with the team, but left after only four races. Lake Speed took the seat and drove for 20 races, leaving the team in September after the Martinsville race. Lake had qualified the Pontiac in the top 10 four times, with his best finish an 11th at Bristol. Chuck Bown, Randy LaJoie, and Dorsey Schroeder all had a chance in the car to finish out the season.

Cale chose Ford for the '92 season, with Chad Little at the wheel for six races before moving to the Melling team for the rest of the season. Bobby Hillin Jr. drove at North Wilkesboro, then handed the wheel to Jimmy Hensley. The team worked hard to give him the best car possible, and there was only one race of the 22 Jimmy contested that was cut short by mechanical problems. He managed four top 10 finishes, winning more than $247,000 before leaving the team at the end of the season.

Cale started the '93 season with Bojangles' sponsorship, and hired Derrike Cope to pilot the #98 Ford for the entire season. He finished in the top 10 once on his way to a 26th place finish in the championship points race.

Fingerhut colors were on the Ford when Cope began the 1994 season. In the first 16 races, the best finish he could muster was a 16th at Darlington, and he was released, eventually finding another ride in a Bobby Allison–owned car. Jeremy Mayfield drove for the balance of the year, only capturing three top 20 finishes.

Mayfield returned for the 1995 season, with RCA sponsorship. The team again put a reliable car on the track, as they only had to leave two races early for the season. Mayfield finished eighth in Pocono, and earned purse money of more than $436,000. He began the '96 season with greater success. He finished fifth in Atlanta, managed a fourth at Martinsville, and put the #98 Ford on the pole at Talladega. He left the team after the September Darlington race to drive for Michael Kranefuss, whose driver, John Andretti, joined Cale and the RCA team for the balance of the season. Andretti added two more qualifying efforts in the top 10, and a fifth place finish at Martinsville.

The 1997 race effort would be the best Cale's team would ever run. Andretti drove the Ford to seven top 10 qualifying spots, including a pole at Talladega. The Pepsi 400 in Daytona yielded the only victory Cale's team would ever enjoy. Andretti led 113 laps in his winning effort. Only three races were stunted by problems, and Andretti broke the $1 million mark in winnings, earning more than $1.1 million, and finishing 23rd in points. RCA pulled away from the sport at the end of the season, and Andretti left the team to drive for Petty Enterprises.

Thorn Apple Valley signed on as the sponsor for the '98 effort, with Greg Sacks as the driver. Greg crashed at Texas, sustaining neck injuries that ended his season. Rich Bickle was hired to drive the remaining 21 races and pulled out a fourth place finish in Martinsville. Bickle resigned to drive for Tyler Jet Motorsports, and Thorn Apple Valley ran into financial difficulties that ended its sponsorship.

Cale felt he was spending more time searching for money than he was racing, so he put the team up for sale.

After closing the shop for a short while, Cale partnered with Wayne Burdette, and they hired Rick Mast to run the 1999 season, even though they had no primary sponsors. Sonic drive-ins sponsored the car at Daytona, and Hobas Pipe signed on for Richmond and Charlotte. Burdette decided to dissolve the partnership, so Cale searched and found Universal Studios/Woody Woodpecker as a primary sponsor for the balance of the season. Mast qualified the #98 Ford in the top 10 at Darlington, Pocono, and Charlotte, finished ninth at New Hampshire, and earned more than $1.29 million. Mast had finished every race entered, the second driver to do so since Cale had performed the feat in 1977.

Mast left the team at the end of the season to drive for Larry Hedrick Motorsports. Universal Studios decided to withdraw sponsorship, leaving Cale with the monumental task of starting over again. He had begun to tire of the endless searching for the sponsorship necessary to fund a team. Each year the costs were rising higher and higher, and even though the purse money grew as well, the numbers were not proportional. Cale felt he was spending more time searching for money than he was racing, so he put the team up for sale. There were several potential deals discussed, but none came to fruition, so he closed the doors in January 2000. The team was sold to Chip MacPherson in the summer of 2000, ending Cale's NASCAR career after 43 years.

CHAPTER 7

The Legend

Merriam-Webster defines the word "legend" as "a popular myth of recent origin." This story of Cale Yarborough transcends the definition of the word in many ways, but there is not another word in the English language that can fully describe the impact of this extraordinary man. Rarely has there been such a combination of attributes as his, and even more rare that a man uses his skills, knowledge, and cunning to reach for one goal throughout his life and achieve it beyond all expectations.

Cale's story is an example of achieving the American dream in a sport that is as American as the stars and stripes. Rising from the sandy farmland in rural America to become a name on the tongues of so many across the nation—and even the world—and to do so using powers embodied within himself speaks of the American spirit. Many of us were instilled with the same values as Cale, but few of us have ever used those values to the fullest the way he did. Racing was not a birthright for Cale—it was a dream. He had no footsteps to follow, but he did have the courage and determination to make his own way, learning as he went, and filing away what he had learned for use whenever he needed it. He knew he could not go it completely alone, so he enlisted the skills of others as he saw fit. He developed a keen sense of how to blend their skills with his own to construct the best situation and to help him reach his goals. He became quite adept at reaching into his bag of tricks and using any tool he could find available to get a job done.

Racing was not a birthright for Cale, it was a dream.

As you can see, his story is not completely one of success. Beginning early in his life, he handled adversity with a single-mindedness few can match. His determination to win that first soap box derby race and then falling short on his first run, the loss of the high school football state championship after envisioning the trophy in his hand, the return trip of the turkeys that had gone to market, Ford pulling out of racing just when it looked as if he was headed straight for the top—all of these situations and more served only to strengthen his resolve. Even one of those setbacks would throw most into a tailspin and would alter their goals and visions, but not Cale. He believed in himself, and that belief carried him to greatness.

It might seem that all this focus could lead to a self-centered personality. Not so with Cale, who was always there for his friends, and especially for his family. How many of us, at the height of our accomplishments, could give up half or more of our paid endeavors to let those who are closest to us know just how much they mean to us? Cale did just that, choosing to race half the schedule shortly after being the only man in history to win three championships in a row, enabling him to be at home more often, to be there when his girls needed him. Of course, they all benefited—Cale by building the type of family bond he had been taught by his own family, and the girls, who could follow his example in their lives and pass it down to another generation.

Without the love, support, and faith his family provided, none of his accomplishments would have been achieved—certainly not on the same level or quality. They always cheered him on, encouraging him to take the next step, assuring him that they would walk it with him. Cale could fall flat on his face, and they would be there to pick him up, dust him off, and send him back on his way.

How much does luck figure into a lifetime? Looking back on specific incidents that helped form Cale's life, it would be easy to pass them off one by one as being controlled by luck. But, as Cale recalls, he always believed that a person makes his own luck. Usually, the luck he encountered was an indirect product of hard work. Hard work was a staple of the Yarborough household when he was growing up.

Farmers never stop, as their crops and animals cannot go untended. Cale lets that same work ethic spill over into every corner of his existence. He applies himself fully into every business venture, every farm task, every kindness he offers a friend or the community. He recognizes true need, and wherever he can, he addresses it. He has also seen the seedier side of people and knows how to sort true needs from greed. You would have to be pretty slick to pull one over on Cale Yarborough.

> **He applies himself fully into every business venture, every farm task, every kindness he offers a friend or the community.**

If luck played a part, it was probably concerning the crashes. Cale watched in horror too many times as a friend lost his life or his career as the result of crashing. He had seen his share, but never found himself involved in catastrophe. He had been beaten and banged up, sore from head to toe, but was always ready to start the next race. True grit and stoicism enabled him to set the pain aside when necessary. There was even a time when he went directly from a wheelchair to the driver's seat, but he didn't let it faze him, and he won the race. Skill helped him to avoid many crashes, but in the ones he could not avoid, maybe luck was a factor.

Physical conditioning has become *de rigueur* with today's racers, with most having fitness coaches and regular regimens of exercise and diet. Cale developed his own program when he first joined the high school football team. It only took one day of running one wind sprint after another for him to decide he needed to be in shape. He didn't have a personal trainer, as they were unheard of in the day, but he found ways on the farm to achieve the same benefits. He got himself into shape then, and has kept himself in shape for his entire life. Careful not to adopt habits to the contrary, he has maintained his weight throughout his life and, even in his late sixties, is still fit as a fiddle. It must work for him—to this day, he takes no daily medications.

> **No matter which direction Cale's life might have turned, it is almost certain that he would have risen to the top of the field.**

To view a testament to his stability of character, all one has to do is visit the man—chances are there will be a friend close by. Not just any friend, but probably one who has been around for much of his lifetime. If you become Cale's friend, it is a status you can expect to keep forever. Many of the residents around Timmonsville and Sardis have called that area home for generations. Their ideals are much the same as his, and they have been able to share and perfect those ideals together. One thing is certain—if you have been in the area for any length of time, you know Cale Yarborough and his reputation as a person.

No matter which direction Cale's life might have turned, it is almost certain that he would have risen to the top of the field. Race fans just happen to be the fortunate ones who could watch with wonder as he performed on the track. He was an artisan, elevating his craft to a new level. His area of expertise was behind the wheel of a race car, any race car. His office was a track with 40 cars vying for the same position. He used his expertise to take that position from them. He was good enough at it to be recognized by his peers as one of the best. His tenacity and determination was a step above most, two tools that helped to propel him into the spotlight.

Any time he would pull out onto the track for a race, he knew that it was a new day. Every driver has his good runs and his bad runs, and, week to week, the dominant driver might change. This week Richard Petty might be the dominant driver. Next week it might be David Pearson, Bobby Allison, Dale Earnhardt, or Darrell Waltrip. The one constant would be that Cale was in the mix. There has never been a driver with a better overall record for the races he was able to complete. Any time he was on any track, if his equipment could handle the stresses of the day, he would finish near the front. Patience was not his greatest virtue until his career reached maturity. Once he had control of his patience, his record soared, mainly because it allowed him to finish races, and you can't win if you don't finish.

There are many good drivers in the sport today, and many of them might be as good as Cale and the drivers of his era. The changes in the sport make it difficult to discern. The level of talent is the same, but some of the talents necessary are different. Cale began in the sport when stock cars were just that. They were cars that could be driven to and from the track, if necessary. As the cars have evolved into sophisticated pieces of machinery, the drivers have progressed in parallel. As Cale began, suspension setup, specialized engine power characteristics, and safety equipment were rudimentary. Drivers would adapt their style of driving specifically for how the car was reacting that day. Cale possessed real talent for this adaptation, and even if he was piloting mediocre equipment, he could wring every last ounce of performance from it. Often he would finish races ahead of cars that were much better than his, but his driving made the difference.

Speed was always Cale's friend, and as the sport progressed, the speeds became greater and greater. The daredevil attitude that he had developed as a youth rose to the surface every time he entered a turn faster than ever before, and his seat-of-the-pants feel for the car enabled him to challenge the new territory he was exploring. He loved the shot of adrenaline these situations produced, and the feeling of accomplishment he encountered, sometimes several times per lap. Running the first lap at Daytona at over 200 mph was a phenomenal accomplishment, and nobody was better suited for it than Cale.

Fame and fortune had always been a part of the equation for Cale. He recognized in his very first experience at the old outlaw tracks that only the best drivers made good in racing, and he decided from the start that he wanted to be the best. He would not and could not settle for less. His plan was directly on target, as the results attest. His fan-friendly nature led to a long-lasting fan base. And his fans were not only in the stands. Other drivers fortunate enough to line up with him on the track could see that he had special assets, and would try to follow and learn from him. Following was all right with Cale, because, in his estimation, any finish less than a win was a loss. Even if a race was cut short by mechanical failure or a crash, his aim was to leave the track feeling that he had given it all he had.

During his illustrious career of 560 races, Cale compiled a record 83 wins, 319 top 10 finishes, and 69 pole positions starts. These statistics are still quite impressive some 25 years after they were achieved. As tributes to his achievements on and off the track, Cale has been recognized by many. The following list of honors represents some of the most notable: 1993 International Motorsports Hall of Fame, 1994 National Motorsports Press Association Hall of Fame Inductee, 1994 Motorsports Hall of Fame Inductee, 1996 Court of Legends Inductee at Charlotte Motor

Speedway, and being named one of NASCAR's 50 Greatest Drivers (1998). Many of the tracks have tributes to Cale's conquests.

Perhaps one of the greatest testaments to Cale's domination is that almost any broadcast of a Nextel Cup race today, no matter the network, contains some reference to Cale and his hard-charging style.

Another reason the term "legend" seems somewhat inappropriate is the part of the definition that deals with the mythical. There is nothing mythical about Cale or any of his accomplishments. They were all genuine, hard-earned, and deserved, but still as spectacular as any myths. It doesn't seem possible to win

During his illustrious career of 560 races, Cale compiled a record 83 wins, 319 top 10 finishes, and 69 pole positions starts.

so many races entered, especially during the late 1970s, and yet it happened. Many of his experiences—the plane crash, the alligator wrestling, the snakebite, the high diving, the parachuting, and the like—sound like stories attributed to mythical figures, but Cale actually lived them all.

His life would not be complete without a good family, and Cale's is an example beyond reproach. Betty Jo was the perfect choice for a wife. Their love for each other is real, and is evident in their eyes as they look at each other. Cale still admits that she is the best thing that ever happened to him. She bore him three beautiful daughters. The days they were born were the best days of his life. He had crossed the finish line first many times, but the feelings he had the days his daughters were born surpassed the joy of winning by leaps and bounds. He is so proud of each of them, and centers his life around them.

The family has grown, and each daughter has graced him with two grandchildren. Julie married William "Bo" Wilhelm, whose family was from Hartsville, and still resides near her father's farm. She has two children, Byerly, who is 19, and Julian, who is eight. Kelly became an attorney and moved to Columbia, South Carolina. She is married to Anthony Woody, and they have a son, Caleb, 11, and a daughter Katherine, who is seven. Cale's youngest daughter, B.J., resides in Mt. Pleasant, South Carolina, near Charleston, with her husband, Gray Sweeney, and their two children, Annie Gray, six, and Will, three.

The family remains extremely close, communicating almost every day. They often meet on weekends at Cale's house on the Santee Cooper Lake, where they enjoy water sports, fishing, and spending time together.

Cale is quite happy to work on the farm. He bought a plantation called Cypress Branch parcel by parcel until he had the whole 4,000 acres. He built a very nice brick ranch on the property in 1981, where he still lives today with Betty Jo and their two dogs.

Dede, the black Labrador, follows him about the property, offering companionship as Cale works on first one project, then another. Some time back, he cleared several acres of dense woods around the branch running behind the house and dug a lake substantial enough for a pontoon boat. There are more than 50 cypress trees that dot the area around the water, giving it an idyllic South Carolina charm. Currently, he has undertaken to expand the lake, and if weather permits, you can probably find him on a 50-year-old tractor, digging the lake out, loading the dirt on a dump truck, and depositing it on a pile that resembles the piles of dirt associated with building a major highway. Cale remembers, as a boy, hearing people say, "Don't work yourself to death." He has come to realize that the statement is completely false.

"You can't work yourself to death, but you can work yourself to life," he says.

"You can't work yourself to death, but you can work yourself to life," is his mantra for a long and productive life.

"I'm just not happy unless I can start when the sun comes up and give it my all until it goes down," he will tell you. "When I can do that, I've had a good day."

APPENDIX

NASCAR Grand National/ Winston Cup

1957

Race	Site	Cars	St	Fin	#	Sponsor / Owner	Car	Laps	Money	Status	Led
40	Darlington	50	44	42	30	Bob Weatherly	Pontiac	31/364	100	rf hub	0

1 start, 31 of 364 laps completed (8.5%), 0 laps led

Win:	0 (0.0%)	Average start: 44.0	Total Winnings: $100
Top 5:	0 (0.0%)	Average finish: 42.0	(excluding bonuses)
Top 10:	0 (0.0%)	DNF: 1	

1959

Race	Site	Cars	St	Fin	#	Sponsor / Owner	Car	Laps	Money	Status	Led
36	Darlington	50	33	27	30	Bob Weatherly	Ford	219/364	150	tires	0

1 start, 219 of 364 laps completed (60.2%), 0 laps led

Win:	0 (0.0%)	Average start: 33.0	Total Winnings: $150
Top 5:	0 (0.0%)	Average finish: 27.0	(excluding bonuses)
Top 10:	0 (0.0%)	DNF: 1	

NASCAR Grand National/Winston Cup (Continued)

1960

Race	Site	Cars	St	Fin	#	Sponsor / Owner	Car	Laps	Money	Status	Led
6	Charlotte	21	20	14	30	Bob Weatherly	Ford	114/200	85	rear end	*

1 start, 114 of 200 laps completed (57.0%), Laps led unknown

Win:	0 (0.0%)	Average start: 20.0	Total Winnings: $85
Top 5:	0 (0.0%)	Average finish: 14.0	(excluding bonuses)
Top 10:	0 (0.0%)	DNF: 1	

1961

Race	Site	Cars	St	Fin	#	Sponsor / Owner	Car	Laps	Money	Status	Led
42	Darlington	43	19	30	52	Julian Buesink	Ford	135/364	200	engine	0

1 start, 135 of 364 laps completed (37.1%), 0 laps led

Win:	0 (0.0%)	Average start: 19.0	Total Winnings: $200
Top 5:	0 (0.0%)	Average finish: 30.0	(excluding bonuses)
Top 10:	0 (0.0%)	DNF: 1	

1962

Race	Site	Cars	St	Fin	#	Sponsor / Owner	Car	Laps	Money	Status	Led
4	Daytona	25	18	10	52	Julian Buesink	Ford	38/40	140	running	0

NASCAR Grand National/Winston Cup (Continued)

1962 (Continued)

Race	Site	Cars	St	Fin	#	Sponsor / Owner	Car	Laps	Money	Status	Led
5	Daytona	48	21	48	52	Julian Buesink	Ford	4/200	400	electrical	0
21	Darlington	32	17	13	52	Julian Buesink	Ford	205/219	600	running	0
24	Atlanta	46	23	40	92	Julian Buesink	Ford	89/219	200	engine	0
45	Darlington	44	25	38	92	Don Harrison	Ford	39/364	650	overheating	0
49	Augusta	16	3	13	92	Don Harrison	Ford	56/200	110	fuel pump	0
52	Charlotte	44	39	25	9	Wildcat Williams	Ford	212/267	375	wheel bearing	0
53	Atlanta	44	31	33	92	Don Harrison	Ford	84/267	250	engine	0

8 starts, 727 of 1,776 laps completed (40.9%), 0 laps led

Win:	0 (0.0%)	Average start: 22.1
Top 5:	0 (0.0%)	Average finish: 27.5
Top 10:	1 (12.5%)	DNF: 6

Total Winnings: $2,725
(excluding bonuses)

1963

Race	Site	Cars	St	Fin	#	Sponsor / Owner	Car	Laps	Money	Status	Led
6	Daytona	31	21	20	52	Julian Buesink	Ford	37/40	75	overheating	0
23	Darlington	31	22	11	52	Julian Buesink	Ford	211/220	600	running	0
26	Charlotte	44	41	23	18	Toy Bolton	Pontiac	336/400	500	running	0

NASCAR Grand National/Winston Cup (Continued)

1963 (Continued)

	Race Site	Cars	St	Fin	#	Sponsor / Owner	Car	Laps	Money	Status	Led
29	Daytona	35	35	34	97	Lewis Osborne	Chevrolet	9/160	250	engine	0
30	Myrtle Beach	18	6	5	19	Herman Beam	Ford	185/200	275	running	0
31	Savannah	15	7	5	19	Herman Beam	Ford	198/200	275	running	0
37	Bristol	36	22	14	19	Herman Beam	Ford	471/500	300	running	0
38	Greenville	21	13	15	19	Herman Beam	Ford	123/200	85	running	0
39	Nashville	21	13	8	19	Herman Beam	Ford	335/350	375	running	*
40	Columbia	22	10	8	19	Herman Beam	Ford	196/200	175	running	0
41	Weaverville	27	16	14	19	Herman Beam	Ford	434/500	275	running	0
42	Spartanburg	17	8	5	19	Herman Beam	Ford	195/200	275	running	*
45	Darlington	41	21	17	19	Herman Beam	Ford	306/364	500	running	0
46	Hickory	26	15	10	19	Herman Beam	Ford	210/250	140	running	0
47	Richmond	26	14	11	19	Herman Beam	Ford	270/300	225	running	0
48	Martinsville	36	19	12	19	Herman Beam	Ford	474/500	300	running	0
49	Moyock	15	6	6	19	Herman Beam	Ford	288/300	225	running	0
52	Charlotte	40	25	12	19	Herman Beam	Ford	251/267	675	running	0

18 starts, 4,529 of 5,151 laps completed (87.9%), Laps led unknown

Win: 0 (0.0%)   Average start: 17.4   Total Winnings: $5,525

NASCAR Grand National/Winston Cup (Continued)

1963 (Continued)

Race	Site	Cars	St	Fin	#	Sponsor / Owner	Car	Laps	Money	Status	Led
	Top 5:	3 (16.7%)				Average finish: 12.8		(excluding bonuses)			
	Top 10:	7 (38.9%)				DNF: 2					

1964

Race	Site	Cars	St	Fin	#	Sponsor / Owner	Car	Laps	Money	Status	Led
2	Augusta	36	24	15	19	Herman Beam	Ford	119/139	650	running	0
7	Daytona	23	13	11	19	Herman Beam	Ford	38/40	150	running	0
8	Daytona	46	22	17	19	Herman Beam	Ford	187/200	1,000	running	0
9	Richmond	27	18	16	19	Herman Beam	Ford	218/250	125	crash	0
10	Bristol	36	19	12	19	Herman Beam	Ford	477/500	400	running	0
13	Atlanta	39	37	24	92	Ray Osborne	Ford	74/334	540	gas leak	0
14	Weaverville	24	10	18	19	Herman Beam	Ford	79/200	100	engine	0
18	North Wilkesboro	31	11	23	19	Herman Beam	Ford	220/400	175	engine	0
19	Martinsville	33	9	7	19	Herman Beam	Plymouth	474/500	575	running	0
20	Savannah	12	7	5	19	Herman Beam	Ford	185/200	275	lug bolts	0
21	Darlington	32	15	19	19	Herman Beam	Ford	172/219	350	running	0
25	Charlotte	44	18	28	19	Herman Beam	Ford	117/400	650	crash	0

NASCAR Grand National/Winston Cup (Continued)

1964 (Continued)

Race	Site	Cars	St	Fin	#	Sponsor / Owner	Car	Laps	Money	Status	Led
26	Greenville	22	3	9	19	Herman Beam	Ford	189/199	150	running	0
27	Asheville	19	5	5	19	Herman Beam	Ford	293/300	275	running	0
29	Concord	19	3	14	19	Herman Beam	Ford	41/200	100	overheating	10
32	Birmingham	20	6	6	19	Herman Beam	Ford	193/200	240	running	0
33	Valdosta	23	4	22	19	Herman Beam	Ford	13/200	100	rear end	0
34	Spartanburg	21	8	7	19	Herman Beam	Ford	179/200	200	crash	0
45	Weaverville	36	5	20	00	Holman-Moody	Ford	267/500	250	radiator	0
51	Darlington	44	14	8	06	Holman-Moody	Ford	344/364	1,525	running	0
55	Hillsboro	28	20	22	31	Tom Spell	Ford	41/167	100	crash	0
56	Martinsville	40	9	10	00	Holman-Moody	Ford	489/500	415	running	0
58	North Wilkesboro	32	9	6	00	Holman-Moody	Ford	389/400	525	running	0
59	Charlotte	44	13	19	00	Holman-Moody	Ford	192/267	425	crash	0

24 starts, 4,990 of 6,879 laps completed (72.5%), 10 laps led

Win:	0 (0.0%)	Average start: 12.6	Total Winnings: $9,295
Top 5:	2 (8.3%)	Average finish: 14.3	(excluding bonuses)
Top 10:	9 (37.5%)	DNF: 12	

1965

Race	Site	Cars	St	Fin	#	Sponsor / Owner	Car	Laps	Money	Status	Led
3	Daytona	28	14	21	10	Gary Weaver	Ford	0/40	100	crash	0
4	Daytona	43	32	9	10	Gary Weaver	Ford	128/133	1,500	running	0
5	Spartanburg	16	10	13	10	Gary Weaver	Pontiac	38/200	110	differential	0
6	Weaverville	21	5	3	10	Gary Weaver	Ford	197/200	450	running	0
7	Richmond	22	14	15	10	Gary Weaver	Ford	124/250	150	differential	0
8	Hillsboro	23	21	21	08	Tom Spell	Ford	22/167	100	engine	0
9	Atlanta	44	44	19	35	Lester Hunter	Dodge	193/334	550	crash	0
10	Greenville	25	8	22	31	Sam Fogle	Ford	16/200	100	engine	0
11	North Wilkesboro	34	15	27	31	Sam Fogle	Ford	88/400	150	oil pressure	0
12	Martinsville	36	20	18	31	Sam Fogle	Ford	384/500	440	running	0
13	Columbia	18	10	10	31	Sam Fogle	Ford	113/124	140	running	3
14	Bristol	33	13	17	31	Sam Fogle	Ford	359/500	320	overheating	0
15	Darlington	31	29	24	10	Gary Weaver	Ford	82/219	300	crash	3
17	Winston-Salem	20	18	8	31	Sam Fogle	Ford	185/200	165	running	0
18	Hickory	24	9	7	31	Sam Fogle	Ford	235/250	200	running	0
19	Charlotte	44	4	22	7	Banjo Matthews	Ford	232/400	1,075	crash	0
20	Shelby	20	19	20	78	Herman Beam	Ford	12/200	100	oil pressure	0
22	Harris	22	6	21	31	Sam Fogle	Ford	10/334	100	clutch	0
23	Nashville	15	7	9	31	Sam Fogle	Ford	78/200	150	driveshaft	0

NASCAR Grand National/Winston Cup (Continued)

1965 (Continued)

Race	Site	Cars	St	Fin	#	Sponsor / Owner	Car	Laps	Money	Status	Led
24	Birmingham	16	9	6	31	Sam Fogle	Ford	107/108	240	running	0
25	Atlanta	42	11	13	06	Kenny Myler	Ford	249/267	655	running	0
26	Greenville	20	6	15	06	Kenny Myler	Ford	62/200	100	crash	0
27	Myrtle Beach	22	4	4	06	Kenny Myler	Ford	193/200	300	running	0
28	Valdosta	21	5	1	06	Kenny Myler	Ford	200/200	1,000	running	18
29	Daytona	40	3	17	27	Banjo Matthews	Ford	108/160	515	engine	72
30	Manassas	24	6	4	06	Kenny Myler	Ford	393/400	350	running	0
31	Old Bridge	20	14	20	31	Sam Fogle	Ford	18/200	100	engine	0
32	Islip	22	7	4	06	Kenny Myler	Ford	245/250	300	running	0
33	Watkins Glen	19	8	4	06	Kenny Myler	Ford	63/66	415	running	0
34	Bristol	36	4	22	27	Banjo Matthews	Ford	183/500	285	engine	0
37	Weaverville	27	13	5	06	Kenny Myler	Ford	487/500	800	running	0
39	Spartanburg	23	6	2	06	Kenny Myler	Ford	198/200	600	running	0
40	Augusta	24	6	6	06	Kenny Myler	Ford	194/200	240	running	0
41	Columbia	23	10	5	06	Kenny Myler	Ford	197/200	275	running	0
42	Moyock	18	8	16	06	Kenny Myler	Ford	90/300	100	alternator	0
43	Beltsville	19	5	11	06	Kenny Myler	Ford	58/200	130	overheating	0

NASCAR Grand National/ Winston Cup (Continued)

1965 (Continued)

Race	Site	Cars	St	Fin	#	Sponsor / Owner	Car	Laps	Money	Status	Led
44	Winston-Salem	20	7	5	06	Kenny Myler	Ford	240/250	275	running	0
45	Darlington	44	9	30	27	Banjo Matthews	Ford	118/364	830	crash	2
47	New Oxford	28	7	7	06	Kenny Myler	Ford	186/200	200	running	0
48	Manassas	30	16	17	06	Kenny Myler	Ford	356/400	115	running	0
49	Richmond	37	17	37	96	Kenny Myler	Ford	28/300	150	overheating	0
50	Martinsville	37	12	24	27	Banjo Matthews	Ford	214/500	325	wheel	0
51	North Wilkesboro	35	6	2	27	Banjo Matthews	Ford	398/400	2,125	running	6
52	Charlotte	44	2	34	27	Banjo Matthews	Ford	47/267	780	engine	27
53	Hillsboro	20	6	4	06	Kenny Myler	Ford	106/112	300	running	0
54	Rockingham	43	7	2	27	Banjo Matthews	Ford	500/500	6,450	running	35

46 starts, 7,734 of 12,295 laps completed (62.9%), 166 laps led

Win:	1 (2.2%)	Average start: 11.1	Total Winnings: $24,155
Top 5:	13 (28.3%)	Average finish: 13.5	(excluding bonuses)
Top 10:	21 (45.7%)	DNF: 23	

NASCAR Grand National/Winston Cup (Continued)

1966

	Race Site	Cars	St	Fin	#	Sponsor / Owner	Car	Laps	Money	Status	Led
1	Augusta	30	9	9	06	Kenny Myler	Ford	291/300	390	running	0
2	Riverside	44	11	26	27	Banjo Matthews	Ford	103/185	650	transmission	0
3	Daytona	33	9	10	27	Banjo Matthews	Ford	40/40	150	running	0
5	Daytona	50	19	2	27	Banjo Matthews	Ford	197/198	12,800	running	33
6	Rockingham	44	8	2	27	Banjo Matthews	Ford	500/500	7,875	running	177
7	Bristol	32	8	24	27	Banjo Matthews	Ford	179/500	300	engine	0
8	Atlanta	44	14	6	27	Banjo Matthews	Ford	329/334	1,250	running	0
9	Hickory	26	22	19	45	Bill Seifert	Ford	121/250	100	overheating	0
12	Winston-Salem	22	16	6	0	Reid Shaw	Ford	195/200	265	running	0
42	Darlington	44	7	11	21	Wood Brothers	Ford	356/364	700	running	33
46	Martinsville	40	7	12	21	Wood Brothers	Ford	464/500	425	differential	0
47	North Wilkesboro	35	6	19	21	Wood Brothers	Ford	355/400	225	engine	0
48	Charlotte	44	6	26	21	Wood Brothers	Ford	207/334	750	wheel bearing	9
49	Rockingham	44	12	4	21	Wood Brothers	Ford	494/500	2,250	running	0

14 starts, 3,831 of 4,605 laps completed (83.2%), 252 laps led

Win:	0 (0.0%)	Average start: 11.0	Total Winnings: $28,130
Top 5:	3 (21.4%)	Average finish: 12.6	(excluding bonuses)

NASCAR Grand National/Winston Cup (Continued)

1966 (Continued)

Race Site	Cars	St	Fin	#	Sponsor / Owner	Car	Laps	Money	Status	Led
Top 10: 7 (50.0%)	DNF: 6									

1967

Race Site	Cars	St	Fin	#	Sponsor / Owner	Car	Laps	Money	Status	Led
4 Daytona	28	2	3	21	Wood Brothers	Ford	40/40	400	running	12
5 Daytona	50	8	39	21	Wood Brothers	Ford	42/200	1,055	suspension	0
7 Bristol	36	7	2	21	Wood Brothers	Ford	500/500	3,050	running	56
10 Atlanta	44	1	1	21	Wood Brothers	Ford	334/334	21,035	running	301
13 North Wilkesboro	34	4	2	21	Wood Brothers	Ford	399/400	2,275	running	0
14 Martinsville	37	4	2	21	Wood Brothers	Ford	500/500	2,300	running	259
20 Charlotte	44	1	41	21	Wood Brothers	Ford	58/400	2,450	steering	24
25 Rockingham	44	4	4	21	Wood Brothers	Ford	496/500	2,650	running	0
28 Daytona	39	2	1	21	Wood Brothers	Ford	160/160	15,725	running	30
33 Bristol	36	3	33	21	Wood Brothers	Ford	59/500	275	engine	0
36 Atlanta	44	9	29	21	Wood Brothers	Ford	132/334	1,150	crash	26
40 Darlington	44	9	44	21	Wood Brothers	Ford	3/364	620	engine	0
45 Martinsville	40	1	28	21	Wood Brothers	Ford	120/500	425	engine	0

NASCAR Grand National/Winston Cup (Continued)

1967 (Continued)

	Race Site	Cars	St	Fin	#	Sponsor / Owner	Car	Laps	Money	Status	Led
46	North Wilkesboro	35	21	7	06	Neil Castles	Dodge	386/400	600	running	0
47	Charlotte	44	1	10	21	Wood Brothers	Ford	301/334	2,100	engine	91
48	Rockingham	44	4	16	21	Wood Brothers	Ford	388/500	700	engine	109
49	Weaverville	30	5	12	16	Bud Moore	Mercury	196/500	375	transmission	0

17 starts, 4,114 of 6,466 laps completed (63.6%), 908 laps led

Win:	2 (11.8%)	Average start: 5.1	Total Winnings: $57,185
Top 5:	7 (41.2%)	Average finish: 16.1	(excluding bonuses)
Top 10:	9 (52.9%)	DNF: 9	

1968

	Race Site	Cars	St	Fin	#	Sponsor / Owner	Car	Laps	Money	Status	Led
1	Macon	30	5	21	16	Bud Moore	Mercury	164/500	250	head gasket	0
3	Riverside	44	7	5	21	Wood Brothers	Ford	184/186	2,225	running	0
4	Daytona	50	1	1	21	Wood Brothers	Mercury	200/200	47,250	running	76
5	Bristol	36	3	24	21	Wood Brothers	Ford	237/500	325	rear end	48
7	Atlanta	44	4	1	21	Wood Brothers	Mercury	334/334	20,680	running	172
12	Martinsville	40	3	1	21	Wood Brothers	Mercury	500/500	5,476	running	51

NASCAR Grand National/ Winston Cup (Continued)

1968 (Continued)

Race	Site	Cars	St	Fin	#	Sponsor / Owner	Car	Laps	Money	Status	Led
15	Darlington	34	9	20	21	Wood Brothers	Mercury	222/291	725	engine	4
18	Charlotte	44	3	44	21	Wood Brothers	Mercury	45/255	1,220	crash	44
23	Rockingham	44	5	32	21	Wood Brothers	Mercury	129/500	580	engine	0
25	Daytona	37	4	1	21	Wood Brothers	Mercury	160/160	15,400	running	142
30	Bristol	36	4	2	21	Wood Brothers	Mercury	499/500	2,650	running	1
33	Atlanta	40	2	18	21	Wood Brothers	Mercury	265/334	1,230	crash	46
39	Darlington	44	2	1	21	Wood Brothers	Mercury	364/364	25,415	running	169
40	Hickory	23	4	16	21	Wood Brothers	Ford	168/250	600	crash	0
41	Richmond	28	4	3	21	Wood Brothers	Mercury	299/300	1,210	running	7
42	Beltsville	23	1	18	21	Wood Brothers	Mercury	142/300	120	crash	142
44	Martinsville	40	1	2	21	Wood Brothers	Mercury	497/500	2,700	running	19
45	North Wilkesboro	30	4	5	21	Wood Brothers	Mercury	395/400	625	running	0
47	Charlotte	45	5	5	21	Wood Brothers	Mercury	332/334	3,335	running	1
48	Rockingham	44	1	26	21	Wood Brothers	Mercury	325/500	1,120	engine	92
49	Jefferson	29	3	1	21	Wood Brothers	Mercury	200/200	1,000	running	51

21 starts, 5,661 of 7,408 laps completed (76.4%), 1,065 laps led

Win: 6 (28.6%)   Average start: 3.6   Total Winnings: $134,136

217

NASCAR Grand National/Winston Cup (Continued)

1968 (Continued)

Race	Site	Cars	St	Fin	#	Sponsor / Owner	Car	Laps	Money	Status	Led

Top 5: 12 (57.1%)   Average finish: 11.8 (excluding bonuses)
Top 10: 12 (57.1%)   DNF: 9

1969

Race	Site	Cars	St	Fin	#	Sponsor / Owner	Car	Laps	Money	Status	Led
3	Riverside	44	11	24	21	Wood Brothers	Mercury	81/186	940	engine	0
4	Daytona	27	9	2	21	Wood Brothers	Mercury	50/50	800	running	19
6	Daytona	50	5	38	21	Wood Brothers	Mercury	103/200	2,560	crash	17
7	Rockingham	43	11	3	21	Wood Brothers	Mercury	498/500	4,975	running	65
9	Bristol	30	3	4	21	Wood Brothers	Mercury	494/500	1,275	running	0
10	Atlanta	40	5	1	21	Wood Brothers	Mercury	334/334	21,590	running	308
16	Martinsville	40	3	25	21	Wood Brothers	Mercury	245/500	575	crash	0
18	Darlington	36	1	2	21	Wood Brothers	Mercury	290/291	8,020	running	23
21	Charlotte	44	4	23	21	Wood Brothers	Mercury	307/400	1,600	hub	3
24	Michigan	38	4	1	21	Wood Brothers	Mercury	250/250	17,625	running	38
28	Daytona	40	1	37	21	Wood Brothers	Mercury	22/160	1,265	engine	20
33	Bristol	32	1	24	21	Wood Brothers	Mercury	57/500	1,080	engine	31

218

NASCAR Grand National/ Winston Cup (Continued)

1969 (Continued)

	Race Site	Cars	St	Fin	#	Sponsor / Owner	Car	Laps	Money	Status	Led
36	Atlanta	40	1	7	21	Wood Brothers	Mercury	331/334	2,560	running	97
37	Michigan	44	2	4	21	Wood Brothers	Mercury	165/165	3,675	running	31
41	Darlington	40	1	29	21	Wood Brothers	Mercury	143/230	2,475	crash	81
46	Martinsville	40	2	17	21	Wood Brothers	Mercury	400/500	800	engine	125
48	Charlotte	45	1	25	21	Wood Brothers	Mercury	260/334	1,510	engine	17
51	Rockingham	40	3	29	21	Wood Brothers	Mercury	168/492	750	crash	55
54	College Station	38	4	25	21	Wood Brothers	Mercury	143/250	990	crash	16

19 starts, 4,341 of 6,176 laps completed (70.3%), 946 laps led

Win:	2 (10.5%)	Average start: 3.8	Total Winnings: $75,065
Top 5:	7 (36.8%)	Average finish: 16.8	(excluding bonuses)
Top 10:	8 (42.1%)	DNF: 11	

1970

	Race Site	Cars	St	Fin	#	Sponsor / Owner	Car	Laps	Money	Status	Led
	Daytona	30	1	1	21	Wood Brothers	Mercury	50/50	1,300	running	24
4	Daytona	40	1	37	21	Wood Brothers	Mercury	31/200	7,465	engine	26
6	Rockingham	40	6	2	21	Wood Brothers	Mercury	489/492	9,890	running	91

NASCAR Grand National/Winston Cup (Continued)

1970 (Continued)

Race	Site	Cars	St	Fin	#	Sponsor / Owner	Car	Laps	Money	Status	Led
8	Atlanta	40	1	2	21	Wood Brothers	Mercury	328/328	11,375	running	129
9	Bristol	30	4	3	21	Wood Brothers	Mercury	456/500	2,345	engine	154
10	Talladega	40	21	5	21	Wood Brothers	Mercury	183/188	4,425	running	12
13	Darlington	36	7	13	27	Banjo Matthews	Ford	250/291	1,200	clutch	0
16	Charlotte	40	3	2	21	Wood Brothers	Mercury	398/400	17,080	running	1
18	Martinsville	39	4	3	21	Wood Brothers	Mercury	376/377	3,100	running	0
19	Michigan	40	4	1	21	Wood Brothers	Mercury	200/200	14,675	running	61
24	Daytona	40	1	35	21	Wood Brothers	Mercury	23/160	875	engine	9
28	Bristol	30	1	17	21	Wood Brothers	Mercury	221/500	1,125	crash	143
31	Atlanta	40	4	2	21	Wood Brothers	Mercury	327/328	11,525	running	0
34	Michigan	40	5	10	21	Wood Brothers	Mercury	188/197	1,050	engine	26
35	Talladega	50	9	6	21	Wood Brothers	Mercury	183/188	3,015	running	2
38	Darlington	40	7	20	21	Wood Brothers	Mercury	331/367	1,720	crash	23
44	Charlotte	40	8	40	21	Wood Brothers	Mercury	10/334	890	crash	0
45	Martinsville	30	3	3	21	Wood Brothers	Mercury	498/500	4,100	running	0
47	Rockingham	40	2	1	21	Wood Brothers	Mercury	492/492	20,445	running	205

19 starts, 5,034 of 6,092 laps completed (82.6%), 906 laps led

NASCAR Grand National/Winston Cup (Continued)

1970 (Continued)

Race	Site	Cars	St	Fin	#	Sponsor / Owner	Car	Laps	Money	Status	Led

Win: 3 (15.8%)   Average start: 4.8   Total Winnings: $117,600
Top 5: 11 (57.9%)   Average finish: 10.7   (excluding bonuses)
Top 10: 13 (68.4%)   DNF: 8

1971

Race	Site	Cars	St	Fin	#	Sponsor / Owner	Car	Laps	Money	Status	Led
2	Daytona	33	16	7	3	Ray Fox	Plymouth	49/50	345	running	0
4	Daytona	40	13	33	3	Ray Fox	Plymouth	61/200	1,375	engine	0
10	Atlanta	40	7	29	3	Ray Fox	Plymouth	245/328	1,070	crash	13
42	Charlotte	42	35	28	87	James Mason	Mercury	209/238	1,054	overheating	0

4 starts, 564 of 816 laps completed (69.1%), 13 laps led

Win: 0 (0.0%)   Average start: 17.8   Total Winnings: $3,844
Top 5: 0 (0.0%)   Average finish: 24.2   (excluding bonuses)
Top 10: 1 (25.0%)   DNF: 3

NASCAR Grand National/Winston Cup (Continued)

1972

Race	Site	Cars	St	Fin	#	Sponsor / Owner	Car	Laps	Money	Status	Led
2	Daytona	40	16	6	3	Ray Fox	Plymouth	188/200	4,660	running	0
22	Michigan	40	20	5	98	Hylton Engineering (James Hylton)	Mercury	196/200	2,150	running	0
29	Charlotte	44	6	39	28	Hoss Ellington	Chevrolet	82/334	757	steering	0
30	Rockingham	40	6	6	28	Hoss Ellington	Chevrolet	485/492	2,650	running	9
31	College Station	44	11	9	28	Hoss Ellington	Chevrolet	245/250	1,450	running	0

5 starts, 1,196 of 1,476 laps completed (81.0%), 9 laps led

Win:	0 (0.0%)	Average start: 11.8	Total Winnings: $11,667
Top 5:	1 (20.0%)	Average finish: 13.0	(excluding bonuses)
Top 10:	4 (80.0%)	DNF: 1	

1973

Race	Site	Cars	St	Fin	#	Sponsor / Owner	Car	Laps	Money	Status	Led
1	Riverside	40	8	24	11	Kar Kare (Richard Howard)	Chevrolet	83/191	3,080	transmission	0
2	Daytona	40	3	22	11	Kar Kare (Richard Howard)	Chevrolet	154/200	4,250	engine	25
3	Richmond	30	6	3	11	Kar Kare (Richard Howard)	Chevrolet	497/500	3,450	running	151
4	Rockingham	40	9	2	11	Kar Kare (Richard Howard)	Chevrolet	492/492	10,125	running	0
5	Bristol	30	1	1	11	Kar Kare (Richard Howard)	Chevrolet	500/500	8,030	running	500

NASCAR Grand National/ Winston Cup (Continued)

1973 (Continued)

Race	Site	Cars	St	Fin	#	Sponsor / Owner	Car	Laps	Money	Status	Led
6	Atlanta	40	4	5	11	Kar Kare (Richard Howard)	Chevrolet	321/328	6,575	running	154
7	North Wilkesboro	30	9	6	11	Kar Kare (Richard Howard)	Chevrolet	393/400	2,130	running	0
8	Darlington	40	2	19	11	Kar Kare (Richard Howard)	Chevrolet	275/367	3,080	engine	0
9	Martinsville	34	6	2	11	Kar Kare (Richard Howard)	Chevrolet	500/500	11,500	running	312
10	Talladega	60	4	41	11	Kar Kare (Richard Howard)	Chevrolet	10/188	3,130	crash	0
11	Nashville	28	1	1	11	Kar Kare (Richard Howard)	Chevrolet	420/420	6,755	running	416
12	Charlotte	40	4	3	11	Kar Kare (Richard Howard)	Chevrolet	399/400	11,700	running	15
13	Dover	40	2	2	11	Kar Kare (Richard Howard)	Chevrolet	500/500	10,700	running	125
14	College Station	38	3	4	11	Kar Kare (Richard Howard)	Chevrolet	247/250	6,445	running	0
15	Riverside	40	4	24	11	Kar Kare (Richard Howard)	Chevrolet	114/153	2,755	engine	11
16	Michigan	40	4	6	11	Kar Kare (Richard Howard)	Chevrolet	196/200	3,550	running	3
17	Daytona	40	2	36	11	Kar Kare (Richard Howard)	Chevrolet	65/160	3,190	crash	33
18	Bristol	30	1	19	11	Kar Kare (Richard Howard)	Chevrolet	343/500	2,590	crash	99
19	Atlanta	40	3	2	11	Kar Kare (Richard Howard)	Chevrolet	327/328	10,625	running	111
20	Talladega	50	7	6	11	Kar Kare (Richard Howard)	Chevrolet	185/188	4,715	running	6
21	Nashville	33	1	14	11	Kar Kare (Richard Howard)	Chevrolet	377/420	2,150	running	196
22	Darlington	40	8	1	11	Kar Kare (Richard Howard)	Chevrolet	367/367	23,140	running	277

NASCAR Grand National/Winston Cup (Continued)

1973 (Continued)

	Race Site	Cars	St	Fin	#	Sponsor / Owner	Car	Laps	Money	Status	Led
23	Richmond	34	3	2	11	Kar Kare (Richard Howard)	Chevrolet	498/500	4,425	running	17
24	Dover	40	6	25	11	Kar Kare (Richard Howard)	Chevrolet	347/500	2,720	crash	0
25	North Wilkesboro	30	4	3	11	Kar Kare (Richard Howard)	Chevrolet	400/400	3,475	running	8
26	Martinsville	36	1	2	11	Kar Kare (Richard Howard)	Chevrolet	479/480	12,500	running	366
27	Charlotte	41	2	1	11	Kar Kare (Richard Howard)	Chevrolet	334/334	45,425	running	257
28	Rockingham	43	18	3	11	Kar Kare (Richard Howard)	Chevrolet	491/492	7,925	running	85

28 starts, 9,314 of 10,258 laps completed (90.8%), 3,167 laps led

Win: 4 (14.3%) Average start: 4.5 Total Winnings: $220,135
Top 5: 16 (57.1%) Average finish: 10.0 (excluding bonuses)
Top 10: 19 (67.9%) DNF: 8

1974

	Race Site	Cars	St	Fin	#	Sponsor / Owner	Car	Laps	Money	Status	Led
1	Riverside	35	2	1	11	Kar Kare (Richard Howard)	Chevrolet	191/191	19,325	running	144
2	Daytona	40	4	2	11	Kar Kare (Richard Howard)	Chevrolet	200/200	21,250	running	9
3	Richmond	28	2	3	11	Kar Kare (Richard Howard)	Chevrolet	494/500	5,505	running	104
4	Rockingham	40	1	2	11	Kar Kare (Richard Howard)	Chevrolet	491/492	11,600	running	164

NASCAR Grand National/Winston Cup (Continued)

1974 (Continued)

Race	Site	Cars	St	Fin	#	Sponsor / Owner	Car	Laps	Money	Status	Led
5	Bristol	30	3	1	11	Kar Kare (Richard Howard)	Chevrolet	500/500	8,655	running	367
6	Atlanta	36	9	1	11	Kar Kare (Richard Howard)	Chevrolet	328/328	18,650	running	87
7	Darlington	40	6	5	11	Kar Kare (Richard Howard)	Chevrolet	328/330	6,025	running	0
8	North Wilkesboro	30	2	2	11	Kar Kare (Richard Howard)	Chevrolet	398/400	5,550	running	0
9	Martinsville	30	1	1	11	Kar Kare (Richard Howard)	Chevrolet	500/500	20,000	running	360
10	Talladega	50	5	9	11	Kar Kare (Richard Howard)	Chevrolet	187/188	5,000	running	0
11	Nashville	28	4	14	11	Kar Kare (Richard Howard)	Chevrolet	346/420	585	engine	198
12	Dover	35	3	1	11	Kar Kare (Richard Howard)	Chevrolet	500/500	18,300	running	220
13	Charlotte	40	4	11	11	Kar Kare (Richard Howard)	Chevrolet	382/400	7,375	crash	29
14	Riverside	35	3	1	11	Kar Kare (Richard Howard)	Chevrolet	138/138	17,925	running	89
15	Michigan	36	2	27	11	Kar Kare (Richard Howard)	Chevrolet	78/180	4,065	engine	20
16	Daytona	40	8	3	11	Carling (Junior Johnson)	Chevrolet	160/160	12,187	running	9
17	Bristol	30	3	1	11	Carling (Junior Johnson)	Chevrolet	500/500	7,725	running	310
18	Nashville	30	2	1	11	Carling (Junior Johnson)	Chevrolet	420/420	8,025	running	134
19	Atlanta	36	1	14	11	Carling (Junior Johnson)	Chevrolet	308/328	4,675	running	95
20	Pocono	35	5	3	11	Carling (Junior Johnson)	Chevrolet	192/192	7,350	running	2
21	Talladega	48	8	4	11	Carling (Junior Johnson)	Chevrolet	186/188	8,285	running	2

NASCAR Grand National / Winston Cup (Continued)

1974 (Continued)

Race	Site	Cars	St	Fin	#	Sponsor / Owner	Car	Laps	Money	Status	Led
22	Michigan	36	3	3	11	Carling (Junior Johnson)	Chevrolet	200/200	7,700	running	60
23	Darlington	40	4	1	11	Carling (Junior Johnson)	Chevrolet	367/367	28,000	running	159
24	Richmond	27	4	21	11	Carling (Junior Johnson)	Chevrolet	121/500	2,570	crash	98
25	Dover	40	5	28	11	Carling (Junior Johnson)	Chevrolet	164/500	3,675	engine	0
26	North Wilkesboro	30	2	1	11	Carling (Junior Johnson)	Chevrolet	400/400	9,275	running	275
27	Martinsville	30	7	11	11	Carling (Junior Johnson)	Chevrolet	421/500	7,900	engine	288
28	Charlotte	42	5	23	11	Carling (Junior Johnson)	Chevrolet	206/334	5,847	engine	44
29	Rockingham	36	4	2	11	Carling (Junior Johnson)	Chevrolet	492/492	11,925	running	231
30	Ontario	40	6	3	11	Carling (Junior Johnson)	Chevrolet	200/200	10,125	running	32

30 starts, 9,398 of 10,548 laps completed (89.1%), 3,530 laps led

Win:	10 (33.3%)	Average start:	3.9	Total Winnings: $305,074
Top 5:	21 (70.0%)	Average finish:	6.7	(excluding bonuses)
Top 10:	22 (73.3%)	DNF: 7		

1975

Race	Site	Cars	St	Fin	#	Sponsor / Owner	Car	Laps	Money	Status	Led
2	Daytona	40	6	3	11	Valvoline (Junior Johnson)	Chevrolet	198/200	21,850	running	6

NASCAR Grand National/Winston Cup (Continued)

1975 (Continued)

Race	Site	Cars	St	Fin	#	Sponsor / Owner	Car	Laps	Money	Status	Led
4	Rockingham	31	7	1	11	Russell Bennett (Junior Johnson)	Chevrolet	492/492	17,200	running	261
5	Bristol	23	3	20	11	Johnson Racing (Junior Johnson)	Chevrolet	155/500	2,525	rear end	78
6	Atlanta	36	12	22	11	Jerry Brown (Junior Johnson)	Chevrolet	260/328	4,300	engine	0
7	North Wilkesboro	28	6	2	11	Johnson Racing (Junior Johnson)	Chevrolet	397/400	5,825	running	16
8	Darlington	36	8	36	11	Holly Farms (Junior Johnson)	Chevrolet	15/367	3,675	engine	0
9	Martinsville	30	7	3	11	Holly Farms (Junior Johnson)	Chevrolet	499/500	6,550	running	35
10	Talladega	50	16	40	11	Holly Farms (Junior Johnson)	Chevrolet	19/188	4,130	windshield	0
11	Nashville	28	3	14	11	Holly Farms (Junior Johnson)	Chevrolet	322/420	2,700	engine	273
12	Dover	35	4	27	11	Holly Farms (Junior Johnson)	Chevrolet	295/500	3,700	engine	75
13	Charlotte	40	5	2	11	Holly Farms (Junior Johnson)	Chevrolet	399/400	16,915	running	149
15	Michigan	36	1	4	11	Holly Farms (Junior Johnson)	Chevrolet	199/200	7,180	running	40
16	Daytona	40	12	26	11	Holly Farms (Junior Johnson)	Chevrolet	113/160	4,010	engine	0
17	Nashville	30	3	1	11	Holly Farms (Junior Johnson)	Chevrolet	420/420	7,735	running	385
18	Pocono	35	5	35	11	Holly Farms (Junior Johnson)	Chevrolet	1/200	3,565	crash	0
19	Talladega	50	15	41	11	Holly Farms (Junior Johnson)	Chevrolet	42/188	3,845	engine	1
20	Michigan	36	8	3	11	Holly Farms (Junior Johnson)	Chevrolet	200/200	9,385	running	0
21	Darlington	40	13	19	11	Holly Farms (Junior Johnson)	Chevrolet	298/367	5,215	engine	0

NASCAR Grand National/Winston Cup (Continued)

1975 (Continued)

Race	Site	Cars	St	Fin	#	Sponsor / Owner	Car	Laps	Money	Status	Led
22	Dover	37	7	4	11	Holly Farms (Junior Johnson)	Chevrolet	497/500	7,050	running	104
23	North Wilkesboro	30	4	2	11	Holly Farms (Junior Johnson)	Chevrolet	400/400	5,960	running	172
24	Martinsville	30	1	19	11	Holly Farms (Junior Johnson)	Chevrolet	394/500	8,660	crash	272
25	Charlotte	42	7	19	11	Holly Farms (Junior Johnson)	Chevrolet	282/334	5,440	engine	40
26	Richmond	28	5	26	11	Holly Farms (Junior Johnson)	Chevrolet	155/500	2,495	engine	62
27	Rockingham	37	4	1	11	Holly Farms (Junior Johnson)	Chevrolet	492/492	19,930	running	396
28	Bristol	30	1	20	11	Holly Farms (Junior Johnson)	Chevrolet	283/500	3,160	engine	172
29	Atlanta	36	6	5	11	Holly Farms (Junior Johnson)	Chevrolet	327/328	7,600	running	4
30	Ontario	40	7	4	11	Holly Farms (Junior Johnson)	Chevrolet	199/200	8,825	running	1

27 starts, 7,353 of 9,784 laps completed (75.2%), 2,542 laps led

Win: 3 (11.1%) Average start: 6.5 Total Winnings: $199,425
Top 5: 13 (48.1%) Average finish: 14.8 (excluding bonuses)
Top 10: 13 (48.1%) DNF: 14

1976

Race	Site	Cars	St	Fin	#	Sponsor / Owner	Car	Laps	Money	Status	Led
1	Riverside	35	6	2	11	Holly Farms (Junior Johnson)	Chevrolet	191/191	14,920	running	5

NASCAR Grand National/Winston Cup (Continued)

1976 (Continued)

Race	Site	Cars	St	Fin	#	Sponsor / Owner		Car	Laps	Money	Status	Led
2	Daytona	42	14	42	11	Holly Farms	(Junior Johnson)	Chevrolet	1/200	4,725	engine	0
3	Rockingham	36	8	3	11	Holly Farms	(Junior Johnson)	Chevrolet	490/492	10,665	running	25
4	Richmond	30	5	4	11	Holly Farms	(Junior Johnson)	Chevrolet	388/400	4,745	crash	81
5	Bristol	30	3	1	11	Holly Farms	(Junior Johnson)	Chevrolet	400/400	18,070	running	285
6	Atlanta	36	4	3	11	Holly Farms	(Junior Johnson)	Chevrolet	327/328	17,855	running	103
7	North Wilkesboro	28	5	1	11	Holly Farms	(Junior Johnson)	Chevrolet	400/400	11,125	running	364
8	Darlington	36	6	25	11	Holly Farms	(Junior Johnson)	Chevrolet	171/367	4,065	engine	16
9	Martinsville	30	7	2	11	Holly Farms	(Junior Johnson)	Chevrolet	499/500	10,450	running	113
10	Talladega	40	5	2	11	Holly Farms	(Junior Johnson)	Chevrolet	188/188	19,670	running	13
11	Nashville	30	2	1	11	Holly Farms	(Junior Johnson)	Chevrolet	420/420	8,565	running	398
12	Dover	39	8	27	11	Holly Farms	(Junior Johnson)	Chevrolet	351/500	3,685	engine	243
13	Charlotte	40	3	3	11	Holly Farms	(Junior Johnson)	Chevrolet	399/400	19,220	running	108
14	Riverside	35	6	7	11	Holly Farms	(Junior Johnson)	Chevrolet	93/95	4,310	running	48
15	Michigan	36	6	2	11	Holly Farms	(Junior Johnson)	Chevrolet	200/200	11,845	running	129
16	Daytona	40	2	1	11	Holly Farms	(Junior Johnson)	Chevrolet	160/160	22,215	running	71
17	Nashville	30	3	5	11	Holly Farms	(Junior Johnson)	Chevrolet	418/420	3,615	running	5
18	Pocono	40	1	25	11	Holly Farms	(Junior Johnson)	Chevrolet	171/200	4,215	running	14

NASCAR Grand National/Winston Cup (Continued)

1976 (Continued)

	Race Site	Cars St	Fin	#	Sponsor / Owner	Car	Laps	Money	Status	Led
19	Talladega	40 8	26	11	Holly Farms (Junior Johnson)	Chevrolet	137/188	5,230	running	16
20	Michigan	36 3	2	11	Holly Farms (Junior Johnson)	Chevrolet	200/200	13,705	running	125
21	Bristol	30 2	1	11	Holly Farms (Junior Johnson)	Chevrolet	400/400	10,025	running	373
22	Darlington	40 7	23	11	Holly Farms (Junior Johnson)	Chevrolet	307/367	4,695	running	49
23	Richmond	30 6	1	11	Holly Farms (Junior Johnson)	Chevrolet	400/400	10,300	running	216
24	Dover	36 1	1	11	Holly Farms (Junior Johnson)	Chevrolet	500/500	18,075	running	218
25	Martinsville	30 4	1	11	Holly Farms (Junior Johnson)	Chevrolet	340/340	22,700	running	273
26	North Wilkesboro	30 4	1	11	Holly Farms (Junior Johnson)	Chevrolet	400/400	11,885	running	292
27	Charlotte	40 4	2	11	Holly Farms (Junior Johnson)	Chevrolet	334/334	22,955	running	81
28	Rockingham	36 9	5	11	Holly Farms (Junior Johnson)	Chevrolet	488/492	7,255	running	0
29	Atlanta	36 7	4	11	Holly Farms (Junior Johnson)	Chevrolet	328/328	8,670	running	59
30	Ontario	40 3	23	11	Holly Farms (Junior Johnson)	Chevrolet	168/200	7,785	clutch	68

30 starts, 9,269 of 10,010 laps completed (92.6%), 3,791 laps led

Win:	9 (30.0%)	Average start: 5.1	Total Winnings: $337,240
Top 5:	22 (73.3%)	Average finish: 8.2	(excluding bonuses)
Top 10:	23 (76.7%)	DNF: 5	

230

1977

Race	Site	Cars	St	Fin	#	Sponsor / Owner	Car	Laps	Money	Status	Led
1	Riverside	35	1	2	11	Holly Farms (Junior Johnson)	Chevrolet	119/119	16,220	running	102
2	Daytona	42	4	1	11	Holly Farms (Junior Johnson)	Chevrolet	200/200	63,700	running	137
3	Richmond	30	7	1	11	Holly Farms (Junior Johnson)	Chevrolet	245/245	12,100	running	161
4	Rockingham	36	6	6	11	Holly Farms (Junior Johnson)	Chevrolet	488/492	7,870	running	34
5	Atlanta	42	5	3	11	Holly Farms (Junior Johnson)	Chevrolet	327/328	13,025	running	136
6	North Wilkesboro	29	2	1	11	Holly Farms (Junior Johnson)	Chevrolet	400/400	14,600	running	320
7	Darlington	36	2	16	11	Holly Farms (Junior Johnson)	Chevrolet	330/367	6,650	running	0
8	Bristol	30	1	1	11	Holly Farms (Junior Johnson)	Chevrolet	500/500	23,300	running	496
9	Martinsville	30	5	1	11	Holly Farms (Junior Johnson)	Chevrolet	384/384	21,600	running	243
10	Talladega	41	5	2	11	Holly Farms (Junior Johnson)	Chevrolet	188/188	23,310	running	29
11	Nashville	30	3	2	11	Holly Farms (Junior Johnson)	Chevrolet	420/420	7,965	running	275
12	Dover	36	6	1	11	Holly Farms (Junior Johnson)	Chevrolet	500/500	17,175	running	141
13	Charlotte	40	3	24	11	Holly Farms (Junior Johnson)	Chevrolet	350/400	7,360	running	0
14	Riverside	35	6	3	11	Holly Farms (Junior Johnson)	Chevrolet	95/95	10,475	running	1
15	Michigan	36	4	1	11	Holly Farms (Junior Johnson)	Chevrolet	200/200	20,625	running	106
16	Daytona	41	2	23	11	Holly Farms (Junior Johnson)	Chevrolet	146/160	2,350	running	13
17	Nashville	30	3	4	11	Holly Farms (Junior Johnson)	Chevrolet	417/420	4,965	running	9
18	Pocono	35	6	6	11	Holly Farms (Junior Johnson)	Chevrolet	198/200	7,400	running	1
19	Talladega	40	4	2	11	Holly Farms (Junior Johnson)	Chevrolet	188/188	18,300	running	2

NASCAR Grand National/Winston Cup (Continued)

1977 (Continued)

	Race Site	Cars	St	Fin	#	Sponsor / Owner	Car	Laps	Money	Status	Led
20	Michigan	36	2	5	11	Holly Farms (Junior Johnson)	Chevrolet	200/200	8,100	running	120
21	Bristol	29	1	1	11	Holly Farms (Junior Johnson)	Chevrolet	400/400	12,100	running	299
22	Darlington	40	4	5	11	Holly Farms (Junior Johnson)	Chevrolet	362/367	12,435	running	70
23	Richmond	28	9	4	11	Holly Farms (Junior Johnson)	Chevrolet	400/400	5,950	running	17
24	Dover	40	2	3	11	Holly Farms (Junior Johnson)	Chevrolet	499/500	10,925	running	10
25	Martinsville	30	3	1	11	Holly Farms (Junior Johnson)	Chevrolet	500/500	23,700	running	352
26	North Wilkesboro	26	5	2	11	Holly Farms (Junior Johnson)	Chevrolet	400/400	8,775	running	1
27	Charlotte	41	2	2	11	Holly Farms (Junior Johnson)	Chevrolet	333/334	25,900	running	26
28	Rockingham	36	2	4	11	Holly Farms (Junior Johnson)	Chevrolet	490/492	9,550	running	81
29	Atlanta	40	9	5	11	Holly Farms (Junior Johnson)	Chevrolet	268/268	9,450	running	33
30	Ontario	42	5	3	11	Holly Farms (Junior Johnson)	Chevrolet	200/200	14,285	running	4

30 starts, 9,747 of 9,867 laps completed (98.8%), 3,219 laps led

Win:	9 (30.0%)	Average start: 4.0	Total Winnings: $440,160
Top 5:	25 (83.3%)	Average finish: 4.5	(excluding bonuses)
Top 10:	27 (90.0%)	DNF: 0	

1978

Race	Site	Cars	St	Fin	#	Sponsor / Owner	Car	Laps	Money	Status	Led
1	Riverside	35	4	1	11	First National City Travelers Checks (Junior Johnson)	Oldsmobile	119/119	20,850	running	58
2	Daytona	41	1	2	11	First National City Travelers Checks (Junior Johnson)	Oldsmobile	200/200	41,900	running	43
3	Richmond	30	7	3	11	First National City Travelers Checks (Junior Johnson)	Oldsmobile	399/400	8,050	running	69
4	Rockingham	36	4	18	11	First National City Travelers Checks (Junior Johnson)	Oldsmobile	407/492	6,270	running	36
5	Atlanta	40	1	4	11	First National City Travelers Checks (Junior Johnson)	Oldsmobile	327/328	23,600	running	54
6	Bristol	29	6	4	11	First National City Travelers Checks (Junior Johnson)	Oldsmobile	494/500	6,850	running	0
7	Darlington	36	13	15	11	First National City Travelers Checks (Junior Johnson)	Oldsmobile	321/367	7,345	engine	171
8	North Wilkesboro	29	4	26	11	First National City Travelers Checks (Junior Johnson)	Oldsmobile	120/400	4,365	overheating	2
9	Martinsville	30	2	16	11	First National City Travelers Checks (Junior Johnson)	Oldsmobile	443/500	5,700	running	133

NASCAR Grand National/Winston Cup (Continued)

1978 (Continued)

Race	Site	Cars	St	Fin	#	Sponsor / Owner	Car	Laps	Money	Status	Led
10	Talladega	41	1	1	11	First National City Travelers Checks (Junior Johnson)	Oldsmobile	188/188	34,300	running	81
11	Dover	40	5	2	11	First National City Travelers Checks (Junior Johnson)	Oldsmobile	500/500	15,100	running	1
12	Charlotte	40	2	4	11	First National City Travelers Checks (Junior Johnson)	Oldsmobile	400/400	31,133	running	130
13	Nashville	30	2	1	11	First National City Travelers Checks (Junior Johnson)	Oldsmobile	420/420	11,215	running	420
14	Riverside	35	2	5	11	First National City Travelers Checks (Junior Johnson)	Oldsmobile	94/95	8,400	running	47
15	Michigan	36	3	1	11	First National City Travelers Checks (Junior Johnson)	Oldsmobile	200/200	21,555	running	60
16	Daytona	40	1	2	11	First National City Travelers Checks (Junior Johnson)	Oldsmobile	160/160	18,350	running	56
17	Nashville	29	2	1	11	First National City Travelers Checks (Junior Johnson)	Oldsmobile	420/420	11,240	running	411

NASCAR Grand National/ Winston Cup (Continued)

1978 (Continued)

Race	Site	Cars	St	Fin	#	Sponsor / Owner	Car	Laps	Money	Status	Led
18	Pocono	40	2	26	11	First National City Travelers Checks (Junior Johnson)	Oldsmobile	166/200	6,255	running	4
19	Talladega	41	1	4	11	First National City Travelers Checks (Junior Johnson)	Oldsmobile	188/188	17,850	running	79
20	Michigan	36	3	2	11	First National City Travelers Checks (Junior Johnson)	Oldsmobile	200/200	14,275	running	72
21	Bristol	30	4	1	11	First National City Travelers Checks (Junior Johnson)	Oldsmobile	500/500	15,910	running	327
22	Darlington	40	6	1	11	First National City Travelers Checks (Junior Johnson)	Oldsmobile	367/367	30,175	running	203
23	Richmond	30	10	4	11	First National City Travelers Checks (Junior Johnson)	Oldsmobile	399/400	6,450	running	0
24	Dover	37	8	2	11	First National City Travelers Checks (Junior Johnson)	Oldsmobile	500/500	15,100	running	221
25	Martinsville	30	6	1	11	First National City Travelers Checks (Junior Johnson)	Oldsmobile	500/500	24,950	running	372

NASCAR Grand National/Winston Cup (Continued)

1978 (Continued)

Race	Site	Cars	St	Fin	#	Sponsor / Owner	Car	Laps	Money	Status	Led
26	North Wilkesboro	27	3	1	11	First National City Travelers Checks (Junior Johnson)	Oldsmobile	400/400	14,000	running	19
27	Charlotte	40	2	22	11	First National City Travelers Checks (Junior Johnson)	Oldsmobile	311/334	14,015	running	59
28	Rockingham	36	1	1	11	First National City Travelers Checks (Junior Johnson)	Oldsmobile	492/492	23,360	running	376
29	Atlanta	39	1	8	11	First National City Travelers Checks (Junior Johnson)	Oldsmobile	323/328	9,700	running	67
30	Ontario	40	1	2	11	First National City Travelers Checks (Junior Johnson)	Oldsmobile	200/200	19,700	running	16

30 starts, 9,758 of 10,298 laps completed (94.8%), 3,587 laps led

Win:	10 (33.3%)	Average start:	3.6	Total Winnings: $487,963
Top 5:	23 (76.7%)	Average finish:	6.0	(excluding bonuses)
Top 10:	24 (80.0%)	DNF: 2		

236

1979

Race	Site	Cars	St	Fin	#	Sponsor / Owner	Car	Laps	Money	Status	Led
1	Riverside	35	2	3	11	Busch (Junior Johnson)	Oldsmobile	119/119	12,675	running	3
2	Daytona	41	3	5	11	Busch (Junior Johnson)	Oldsmobile	199/200	34,525	crash	3
3	Rockingham	35	3	18	11	Busch (Junior Johnson)	Oldsmobile	413/492	7,570	running	9
4	Richmond	30	9	1	11	Busch (Junior Johnson)	Oldsmobile	400/400	16,275	running	181
5	Atlanta	40	4	4	11	Busch (Junior Johnson)	Oldsmobile	327/328	11,725	running	22
6	North Wilkesboro	30	2	9	11	Busch (Junior Johnson)	Oldsmobile	397/400	4,925	running	70
7	Bristol	30	5	24	11	Busch (Junior Johnson)	Oldsmobile	216/500	4,470	crash	1
8	Darlington	36	9	6	11	Busch (Junior Johnson)	Oldsmobile	364/367	9,450	running	0
9	Martinsville	30	5	11	11	Busch (Junior Johnson)	Oldsmobile	492/500	5,050	running	0
10	Talladega	39	8	33	11	Busch (Junior Johnson)	Oldsmobile	4/188	6,670	crash	1
11	Nashville	28	4	1	11	Busch (Junior Johnson)	Oldsmobile	420/420	12,275	running	83
12	Dover	31	7	2	11	Busch (Junior Johnson)	Chevrolet	500/500	14,800	running	265
13	Charlotte	41	5	4	11	Busch (Junior Johnson)	Oldsmobile	398/400	18,225	running	0
14	College Station	34	5	4	11	Busch (Junior Johnson)	Chevrolet	199/200	12,150	running	0
15	Riverside	35	6	4	11	Busch (Junior Johnson)	Chevrolet	95/95	11,800	running	57
16	Michigan	36	5	3	11	Busch (Junior Johnson)	Oldsmobile	200/200	12,620	running	4
17	Daytona	41	5	20	11	Busch (Junior Johnson)	Oldsmobile	149/160	6,960	running	0
18	Nashville	30	5	2	11	Busch (Junior Johnson)	Chevrolet	419/420	8,700	running	0
19	Pocono	39	2	1	11	Busch (Junior Johnson)	Chevrolet	200/200	21,465	running	61

NASCAR Grand National/Winston Cup (Continued)

1979 (Continued)

Race	Site	Cars	St	Fin	#	Sponsor / Owner	Car	Laps	Money	Status	Led
20	Talladega	41	5	24	11	Busch (Junior Johnson)	Oldsmobile	138/188	8,015	engine	14
21	Michigan	36	8	17	11	Busch (Junior Johnson)	Chevrolet	185/200	6,270	engine	3
22	Bristol	30	4	5	11	Busch (Junior Johnson)	Chevrolet	497/500	5,600	running	0
23	Darlington	40	11	19	11	Busch (Junior Johnson)	Chevrolet	336/367	8,000	running	0
24	Richmond	26	3	5	11	Busch (Junior Johnson)	Oldsmobile	398/400	5,975	running	0
25	Dover	36	12	3	11	Busch (Junior Johnson)	Chevrolet	500/500	11,250	running	227
26	Martinsville	30	4	8	11	Busch (Junior Johnson)	Oldsmobile	489/500	5,450	running	3
27	Charlotte	40	4	1	11	Busch (Junior Johnson)	Chevrolet	334/334	39,000	running	58
28	North Wilkesboro	29	6	20	11	Busch (Junior Johnson)	Oldsmobile	269/400	4,775	crash	17
29	Rockingham	37	9	3	11	Busch (Junior Johnson)	Chevrolet	492/492	11,800	running	50
30	Atlanta	41	2	3	11	Busch (Junior Johnson)	Oldsmobile	328/328	23,150	running	136
31	Ontario	37	1	3	11	Busch (Junior Johnson)	Oldsmobile	200/200	18,000	running	55

31 starts, 9,677 of 10,498 laps completed (92.2%), 1,323 laps led

Win:	4 (12.9%)	Average start: 5.3	Total Winnings: $379,615
Top 5:	19 (61.3%)	Average finish: 8.6	(excluding bonuses)
Top 10:	22 (71.0%)	DNF: 6	

238

1980

Race	Site	Cars	St	Fin	#	Sponsor / Owner	Car	Laps	Money	Status	Led
1	Riverside	37	2	23	11	Busch (Junior Johnson)	Chevrolet	103/119	5,530	engine	41
2	Daytona	42	5	19	11	Busch (Junior Johnson)	Oldsmobile	183/200	17,150	running	24
3	Richmond	31	9	25	11	Busch (Junior Johnson)	Chevrolet	193/400	4,025	crash	0
4	Rockingham	38	21	1	11	Busch (Junior Johnson)	Oldsmobile	492/492	19,280	running	256
5	Atlanta	41	3	8	11	Busch (Junior Johnson)	Chevrolet	324/328	18,145	running	183
6	Bristol	32	1	5	11	Busch (Junior Johnson)	Chevrolet	498/500	7,100	running	187
7	Darlington	36	3	12	11	Busch (Junior Johnson)	Chevrolet	182/189	7,275	engine	35
8	North Wilkesboro	31	3	4	11	Busch (Junior Johnson)	Chevrolet	397/400	8,475	running	0
9	Martinsville	32	5	4	11	Busch (Junior Johnson)	Chevrolet	500/500	8,750	running	58
10	Talladega	42	3	6	11	Busch (Junior Johnson)	Oldsmobile	186/188	14,300	running	32
11	Nashville	30	1	3	11	Busch (Junior Johnson)	Chevrolet	420/420	8,660	running	279
12	Dover	34	1	16	11	Busch (Junior Johnson)	Chevrolet	411/500	7,800	running	137
13	Charlotte	42	1	17	11	Busch (Junior Johnson)	Chevrolet	379/400	25,200	running	43
14	College Station	31	1	1	11	Busch (Junior Johnson)	Chevrolet	200/200	21,000	running	110
15	Riverside	36	1	4	11	Busch (Junior Johnson)	Chevrolet	95/95	9,650	running	3
16	Michigan	37	2	2	11	Busch (Junior Johnson)	Chevrolet	200/200	16,300	running	37
17	Daytona	40	1	40	11	Busch (Junior Johnson)	Oldsmobile	5/160	7,855	engine	5
18	Nashville	30	1	2	11	Busch (Junior Johnson)	Chevrolet	420/420	10,160	running	151
19	Pocono	40	1	3	11	Busch (Junior Johnson)	Chevrolet	200/200	13,640	running	54

NASCAR Grand National/Winston Cup (Continued)

1980 (Continued)

Race	Site	Cars	St	Fin	#	Sponsor / Owner	Car	Laps	Money	Status	Led
20	Talladega	41	3	2	11	Busch (Junior Johnson)	Oldsmobile	188/188	20,625	running	25
21	Michigan	37	2	1	11	Busch (Junior Johnson)	Chevrolet	200/200	19,700	running	41
22	Bristol	30	1	1	11	Busch (Junior Johnson)	Chevrolet	500/500	16,550	running	379
23	Darlington	41	2	29	11	Busch (Junior Johnson)	Chevrolet	277/367	6,675	running	0
24	Richmond	29	1	26	11	Busch (Junior Johnson)	Oldsmobile	145/400	5,585	cyl head	47
25	Dover	40	1	4	11	Busch (Junior Johnson)	Chevrolet	499/500	10,700	running	30
26	North Wilkesboro	30	1	10	11	Busch (Junior Johnson)	Chevrolet	389/400	11,225	running	54
27	Martinsville	31	2	3	11	Busch (Junior Johnson)	Oldsmobile	500/500	11,975	running	51
28	Charlotte	41	3	2	11	Busch (Junior Johnson)	Chevrolet	334/334	30,200	running	47
29	Rockingham	36	2	1	11	Busch (Junior Johnson)	Chevrolet	492/492	20,160	running	167
30	Atlanta	40	12	1	11	Busch (Junior Johnson)	Chevrolet	328/328	31,600	running	269
31	Ontario	42	1	3	11	Busch (Junior Johnson)	Chevrolet	200/200	17,035	running	65

31 starts, 9,440 of 10,320 laps completed (91.5%), 2,810 laps led

Win:	6 (19.4%)	Average start: 3.1
Top 5:	19 (61.3%)	Average finish: 9.0
Top 10:	22 (71.0%)	DNF: 5

Total Winnings: $432,325
(excluding bonuses)

1981

Race	Site	Cars	St	Fin	#	Sponsor / Owner	Car	Laps	Money	Status	Led
2	Daytona	42	29	8	27	Valvoline (M.C. Anderson)	Oldsmobile	197/200	20,325	running	0
4	Rockingham	37	1	2	27	Valvoline (M.C. Anderson)	Buick	492/492	12,370	running	320
5	Atlanta	42	17	1	27	Valvoline (M.C. Anderson)	Buick	328/328	28,950	running	71
8	Darlington	36	7	26	27	Valvoline (M.C. Anderson)	Buick	233/367	1,650	engine	134
9	Martinsville	31	21	21	27	Valvoline (M.C. Anderson)	Buick	317/500	940	engine	48
10	Talladega	40	8	24	27	Valvoline (M.C. Anderson)	Buick	86/188	2,860	engine	0
12	Dover	32	6	10	27	Valvoline (M.C. Anderson)	Buick	480/500	2,925	engine	32
13	Charlotte	42	2	3	27	Valvoline (M.C. Anderson)	Buick	398/400	22,425	running	0
16	Michigan	37	17	8	27	Valvoline (M.C. Anderson)	Buick	200/200	3,300	running	29
17	Daytona	42	1	1	27	Valvoline (M.C. Anderson)	Buick	160/160	24,625	running	78
19	Pocono	35	10	5	27	Valvoline (M.C. Anderson)	Buick	200/200	4,290	running	2
20	Talladega	42	5	28	27	Valvoline (M.C. Anderson)	Buick	83/188	2,725	crash	6
21	Michigan	36	2	17	27	Valvoline (M.C. Anderson)	Buick	198/200	2,445	running	9
23	Darlington	40	2	10	27	Valvoline (M.C. Anderson)	Buick	363/367	5,925	running	24
25	Dover	34	6	13	27	Valvoline (M.C. Anderson)	Buick	492/500	2,210	running	0
28	Charlotte	41	3	31	27	Valvoline (M.C. Anderson)	Buick	153/334	2,100	engine	2
29	Rockingham	37	8	25	27	Valvoline (M.C. Anderson)	Buick	214/492	1,225	crash	0
30	Atlanta	40	21	3	27	Valvoline (M.C. Anderson)	Buick	328/328	8,800	running	14

18 starts, 4,922 of 5,944 laps completed (82.8%), 769 laps led

NASCAR Grand National/Winston Cup (Continued)

1981 (Continued)

Race Site	Cars	St	Fin	#	Sponsor / Owner	Car	Laps	Money	Status	Led
Win: 2 (11.1%)					Average start: 9.2	Total Winnings: $150,090				
Top 5: 6 (33.3%)					Average finish: 13.1	(excluding bonuses)				
Top 10: 10 (55.6%)					DNF: 7					

1982

#	Race Site	Cars	St	Fin	#	Sponsor / Owner	Car	Laps	Money	Status	Led
1	Daytona	42	3	2	27	Valvoline (M.C. Anderson)	Buick	200/200	70,725	running	5
4	Atlanta	39	15	3	27	Valvoline (M.C. Anderson)	Buick	287/287	16,250	running	20
5	Rockingham	34	11	1	27	Valvoline (M.C. Anderson)	Buick	492/492	17,360	running	51
6	Darlington	37	9	2	27	Valvoline (M.C. Anderson)	Buick	367/367	12,550	running	4
9	Talladega	40	6	37	27	Valvoline (M.C. Anderson)	Buick	17/188	1,635	engine	0
12	Charlotte	42	5	4	27	Valvoline (M.C. Anderson)	Buick	398/400	15,850	running	0
13	Pocono	37	27	28	27	Valvoline (M.C. Anderson)	Buick	92/200	1,200	engine	3
15	Michigan	37	4	1	27	Valvoline (M.C. Anderson)	Buick	200/200	24,700	running	73
16	Daytona	40	5	22	27	Valvoline (M.C. Anderson)	Buick	141/160	2,820	suspension	17
18	Pocono	36	1	26	27	Valvoline (M.C. Anderson)	Buick	128/200	2,900	engine	39
19	Talladega	40	4	4	27	Valvoline (M.C. Anderson)	Buick	188/188	11,625	running	8

NASCAR Grand National/Winston Cup (Continued)

1982 (Continued)

Race	Site	Cars	St	Fin	#	Sponsor / Owner	Car	Laps	Money	Status	Led
20	Michigan	38	7	28	27	Valvoline (M.C. Anderson)	Buick	103/200	1,250	transmission	28
22	Darlington	40	9	1	27	Valvoline (M.C. Anderson)	Buick	367/367	34,300	running	99
26	Charlotte	40	14	33	27	Valvoline (M.C. Anderson)	Buick	98/334	1,640	engine	0
28	Rockingham	35	1	25	27	Valvoline (M.C. Anderson)	Buick	288/492	2,760	crash	32
29	Atlanta	40	19	35	27	Valvoline (M.C. Anderson)	Buick	73/328	775	engine	0

16 starts, 3,439 of 4,603 laps completed (74.7%), 379 laps led

Win:	3 (18.8%)	Average start:	8.8	Total Winnings: $218,340
Top 5:	8 (50.0%)	Average finish:	15.8	(excluding bonuses)
Top 10:	8 (50.0%)	DNF:	8	

1983

Race	Site	Cars	St	Fin	#	Sponsor / Owner	Car	Laps	Money	Status	Led
1	Daytona	42	8	1	28	Hardee's (Harry Ranier)	Pontiac	200/200	119,600	running	23
3	Rockingham	35	5	9	28	Hardee's (Harry Ranier)	Chevrolet	486/492	7,335	running	161
4	Atlanta	41	22	1	28	Hardee's (Harry Ranier)	Chevrolet	328/328	33,300	running	78
5	Darlington	36	14	6	28	Hardee's (Harry Ranier)	Chevrolet	365/367	5,050	running	0
8	Talladega	42	1	29	28	Hardee's (Harry Ranier)	Chevrolet	71/188	5,885	crash	43

NASCAR Grand National/Winston Cup (Continued)

1983 (Continued)

Race	Site	Cars	St	Fin	#	Sponsor / Owner	Car	Laps	Money	Status	Led
10	Dover	36	11	22	28	Hardee's (Harry Ranier)	Chevrolet	350/500	1,150	overheating	0
12	Charlotte	41	12	28	28	Hardee's (Harry Ranier)	Chevrolet	321/400	6,765	engine	31
14	Pocono	38	5	27	28	Hardee's (Harry Ranier)	Chevrolet	150/200	1,750	oil pan	0
15	Michigan	37	9	1	28	Hardee's (Harry Ranier)	Chevrolet	200/200	24,170	running	37
16	Daytona	40	1	40	28	Hardee's (Harry Ranier)	Chevrolet	5/160	3,250	engine	1
19	Talladega	40	1	24	28	Hardee's (Harry Ranier)	Chevrolet	140/188	5,820	engine	21
20	Michigan	37	7	1	28	Hardee's (Harry Ranier)	Chevrolet	200/200	26,100	running	85
22	Darlington	41	15	7	28	Hardee's (Harry Ranier)	Chevrolet	366/367	4,875	running	1
27	Charlotte	40	11	10	28	Hardee's (Harry Ranier)	Chevrolet	333/334	6,650	running	10
28	Rockingham	36	2	36	28	Hardee's (Harry Ranier)	Chevrolet	10/492	1,035	crash	9
29	Atlanta	39	4	23	28	Hardee's (Harry Ranier)	Chevrolet	258/328	1,800	engine	108

16 starts, 3,783 of 4,944 laps completed (76.5%), 608 laps led

Win:	4 (25.0%)	Average start: 8.0
Top 5:	4 (25.0%)	Average finish: 16.6
Top 10:	8 (50.0%)	DNF: 8

Total Winnings: $254,535
(excluding bonuses)

APPENDIX

1984

Race	Site	Cars	St	Fin	#	Sponsor / Owner	Car	Laps	Money	Status	Led
1	Daytona	42	1	1	28	Hardee's (Harry Ranier)	Chevrolet	200/200	160,300	running	89
2	Richmond	32	9	14	28	Hardee's (Harry Ranier)	Chevrolet	396/400	1,665	running	0
4	Atlanta	40	3	3	28	Hardee's (Harry Ranier)	Chevrolet	328/328	12,550	running	90
7	Darlington	38	5	4	28	Hardee's (Harry Ranier)	Chevrolet	366/367	6,850	running	42
9	Talladega	40	1	1	28	Hardee's (Harry Ranier)	Chevrolet	188/188	42,300	running	19
12	Charlotte	42	14	21	28	Hardee's (Harry Ranier)	Chevrolet	383/400	19,125	engine	132
14	Pocono	39	12	1	28	Hardee's (Harry Ranier)	Chevrolet	200/200	30,850	running	64
15	Michigan	40	5	13	28	Hardee's (Harry Ranier)	Chevrolet	199/200	7,250	running	67
16	Daytona	42	1	3	28	Hardee's (Harry Ranier)	Chevrolet	160/160	23,640	running	79
18	Pocono	40	9	2	28	Hardee's (Harry Ranier)	Chevrolet	200/200	17,275	running	56
19	Talladega	40	1	5	28	Hardee's (Harry Ranier)	Chevrolet	188/188	15,350	running	34
20	Michigan	40	9	5	28	Hardee's (Harry Ranier)	Chevrolet	200/200	8,100	running	0
22	Darlington	41	15	17	28	Hardee's (Harry Ranier)	Chevrolet	325/367	3,350	engine	0
23	Richmond	30	12	14	28	Hardee's (Harry Ranier)	Chevrolet	395/400	1,400	running	0
26	Charlotte	41	17	3	28	Hardee's (Harry Ranier)	Chevrolet	334/334	23,258	running	8
29	Atlanta	40	4	11	28	Hardee's (Harry Ranier)	Chevrolet	325/328	12,590	running	56

16 starts, 4,387 of 4,460 laps completed (98.4%), 736 laps led

Win:	3 (18.8%)	Total Winnings: $385,853
Top 5:	10 (62.5%)	(excluding bonuses)

Average start: 7.4
Average finish: 7.4

NASCAR Grand National/Winston Cup (Continued)

1984 (Continued)

Race Site	Cars St	Fin	#	Sponsor / Owner	Car	Laps	Money	Status	Led
1 Daytona	40 2	36	28	Hardee's (Harry Ranier)	Ford	62/200	33,530	engine	32

Top 10: 10 (62.5%)   DNF: 2

1985

Race Site	Cars St	Fin	#	Sponsor / Owner	Car	Laps	Money	Status	Led
3 Rockingham	40 15	7	28	Hardee's (Harry Ranier)	Ford	491/492	4,660	running	0
4 Atlanta	41 4	22	28	Hardee's (Harry Ranier)	Ford	273/328	1,950	engine	111
6 Darlington	40 21	30	28	Hardee's (Harry Ranier)	Ford	164/367	1,975	engine	0
9 Talladega	39 2	3	28	Hardee's (Harry Ranier)	Ford	188/188	37,750	running	97
11 Charlotte	42 7	40	28	Hardee's (Harry Ranier)	Ford	19/400	1,575	engine	0
13 Pocono	40 13	24	28	Hardee's (Harry Ranier)	Ford	176/200	2,080	valve	0
14 Michigan	37 27	3	28	Hardee's (Harry Ranier)	Ford	200/200	16,900	running	0
15 Daytona	41 2	36	28	Hardee's (Harry Ranier)	Ford	24/160	2,500	transmission	4
16 Pocono	40 3	31	28	Hardee's (Harry Ranier)	Ford	127/200	2,195	engine	18
17 Talladega	42 2	1	28	Hardee's (Harry Ranier)	Ford	188/188	48,655	running	41
18 Michigan	40 9	32	28	Hardee's (Harry Ranier)	Ford	118/200	1,370	engine	1
20 Darlington	40 22	2	28	Hardee's (Harry Ranier)	Ford	367/367	22,050	running	25

NASCAR Grand National/Winston Cup (Continued)

1985 (Continued)

Race	Site	Cars	St	Fin	#	Sponsor / Owner	Car	Laps	Money	Status	Led
25	Charlotte	42	7	1	28	Hardee's (Harry Ranier)	Ford	334/334	51,600	running	49
26	Rockingham	40	5	28	28	Hardee's (Harry Ranier)	Ford	391/492	2,075	crash	149
27	Atlanta	42	9	2	28	Hardee's (Harry Ranier)	Ford	328/328	29,600	running	137

16 starts, 3,450 of 4,644 laps completed (74.3%), 664 laps led

Win:	2 (12.5%)	Average start: 9.4	Total Winnings: $260,465
Top 5:	6 (37.5%)	Average finish: 18.6	(excluding bonuses)
Top 10:	7 (43.8%)	DNF: 9	

1986

Race	Site	Cars	St	Fin	#	Sponsor / Owner	Car	Laps	Money	Status	Led
1	Daytona	42	13	27	28	Hardee's (Harry Ranier)	Ford	116/200	12,985	crash	5
3	Rockingham	40	10	6	28	Hardee's (Harry Ranier)	Ford	490/492	5,410	running	0
4	Atlanta	42	6	27	28	Hardee's (Harry Ranier)	Ford	300/328	1,665	oil line	0
6	Darlington	40	23	22	28	Hardee's (Harry Ranier)	Ford	267/367	2,535	engine	0
9	Talladega	42	4	37	28	Hardee's (Harry Ranier)	Ford	63/188	2,575	engine	0
11	Charlotte	41	12	3	28	Hardee's (Harry Ranier)	Ford	400/400	34,375	running	98
13	Pocono	40	10	3	28	Hardee's (Harry Ranier)	Ford	200/200	15,450	running	0

NASCAR Grand National/Winston Cup (Continued)

1986 (Continued)

	Race Site	Cars	St	Fin	#	Sponsor / Owner	Car	Laps	Money	Status	Led
14	Michigan	41	28	30	28	Hardee's (Harry Ranier)	Ford	130/200	1,730	crash	2
15	Daytona	42	1	17	28	Hardee's (Harry Ranier)	Ford	159/160	6,975	running	5
16	Pocono	40	16	25	28	Hardee's (Harry Ranier)	Ford	138/150	2,135	engine	0
17	Talladega	40	19	24	28	Hardee's (Harry Ranier)	Ford	159/188	2,930	crash	0
19	Michigan	41	28	7	28	Hardee's (Harry Ranier)	Ford	199/200	6,815	running	0
21	Darlington	40	8	10	28	Hardee's (Harry Ranier)	Ford	366/367	6,435	running	0
26	Charlotte	42	11	36	28	Hardee's (Harry Ranier)	Ford	84/334	1,490	crash	0
27	Rockingham	40	3	33	28	Hardee's (Harry Ranier)	Ford	200/492	1,425	ignition	0
28	Atlanta	42	13	34	28	Hardee's (Harry Ranier)	Ford	196/328	1,080	engine	0

16 starts, 3,467 of 4,594 laps completed (75.5%), 110 laps led

Win:	0 (0.0%)	Average start: 12.8	Total Winnings: $106,010
Top 5:	2 (12.5%)	Average finish: 21.3	(excluding bonuses)
Top 10:	5 (31.2%)	DNF: 10	

1987

	Race Site	Cars	St	Fin	#	Sponsor / Owner	Car	Laps	Money	Status	Led
1	Daytona	42	22	10	29	Hardee's (Cale Yarborough)	Oldsmobile	200/200	29,600	running	0

248

NASCAR Grand National/Winston Cup (Continued)

1987 (Continued)

Race	Site	Cars	St	Fin	#	Sponsor / Owner	Car	Laps	Money	Status	Led
2	Rockingham	42	24	28	29	Hardee's (Cale Yarborough)	Oldsmobile	339/492	1,815	transmission	0
4	Atlanta	41	3	8	29	Hardee's (Cale Yarborough)	Oldsmobile	327/328	5,650	running	7
5	Darlington	41	21	15	29	Hardee's (Cale Yarborough)	Oldsmobile	354/367	3,715	running	0
9	Talladega	41	18	37	29	Hardee's (Cale Yarborough)	Oldsmobile	22/178	3,100	crash	0
10	Charlotte	42	12	42	29	Hardee's (Cale Yarborough)	Oldsmobile	19/400	1,525	oil line	0
12	Pocono	40	8	4	29	Hardee's (Cale Yarborough)	Oldsmobile	200/200	11,505	running	0
14	Michigan	40	25	33	29	Hardee's (Cale Yarborough)	Oldsmobile	130/200	2,025	brakes	0
15	Daytona	41	27	24	29	Hardee's (Cale Yarborough)	Oldsmobile	155/160	2,805	engine	0
17	Talladega	40	22	5	29	Hardee's (Cale Yarborough)	Oldsmobile	188/188	13,465	running	4
19	Michigan	40	32	40	29	Hardee's (Cale Yarborough)	Oldsmobile	22/200	1,660	engine	0
21	Darlington	40	21	13	29	Hardee's (Cale Yarborough)	Oldsmobile	201/202	4,375	running	0
23	Dover	40	39	36	29	Hardee's (Cale Yarborough)	Oldsmobile	117/500	1,175	engine	0
26	Charlotte	42	25	24	29	Hardee's (Cale Yarborough)	Oldsmobile	214/334	3,565	running	0
27	Rockingham	42	19	37	29	Hardee's (Cale Yarborough)	Oldsmobile	151/492	1,310	engine	0
29	Atlanta	42	6	40	29	Hardee's (Cale Yarborough)	Oldsmobile	32/328	1,235	crash	0

16 starts, 2,671 of 4,769 laps completed (56.0%), 11 laps led

Win: 0 (0.0%)   Average start: 20.2   Total Winnings: $88,525

NASCAR Grand National/Winston Cup (Continued)

1987 (Continued)

Race Site	Cars St	Fin	#	Sponsor / Owner	Car	Laps	Money	Status	Led
Top 5: 2 (12.5%)	Average finish: 24.8			(excluding bonuses)					
Top 10: 4 (25.0%)	DNF: 9								

1988

Race	Site	Cars St	Fin	#	Sponsor / Owner	Car	Laps	Money	Status	Led
1	Daytona	42	32	38	29	Hardee's (Cale Yarborough)	Oldsmobile	46/200	8,780	crash	0
4	Atlanta	42	19	32	29	Hardee's (Cale Yarborough)	Oldsmobile	127/328	2,030	brakes	0
9	Talladega	41	37	18	29	Hardee's (Cale Yarborough)	Oldsmobile	186/188	4,920	running	0
10	Charlotte	41	33	38	29	Hardee's (Cale Yarborough)	Oldsmobile	58/400	1,625	crash	0
14	Michigan	41	28	9	29	Hardee's (Cale Yarborough)	Oldsmobile	199/200	9,700	running	1
15	Daytona	42	25	41	29	Hardee's (Cale Yarborough)	Oldsmobile	1/160	2,765	crash	0
17	Talladega	42	16	9	29	Hardee's (Cale Yarborough)	Oldsmobile	188/188	8,520	running	5
19	Michigan	42	33	18	29	Hardee's (Cale Yarborough)	Oldsmobile	198/200	5,175	running	0
25	Charlotte	42	20	22	29	Hardee's (Cale Yarborough)	Oldsmobile	323/334	4,750	running	0
29	Atlanta	42	26	10	29	Hardee's (Cale Yarborough)	Oldsmobile	327/328	7,800	running	0

10 starts, 1,653 of 2,526 laps completed (65.4%), 6 laps led

Win: 0 (0.0%)   Average start: 26.9   Total Winnings: $56,065

NASCAR Grand National/Winston Cup (Continued)

1988 (Continued)

Top 5:	0 (0.0%)	Average finish: 23.5				
Top 10:	3 (30.0%)	DNF: 4				

Career statistics

	Race	Site	Cars	St	Fin	#	Sponsor / Owner (excluding bonuses)			Car	Laps		Money	Status	Led
1957	18	1 of 53	0	0	0	0	31	0	100	159	44.0	42.0	0	42.6	0
1959	20	1 of 44	0	0	0	0	219	0	150	110	33.0	27.0	0	301.1	0
1960	21	1 of 44	0	0	0	0	114	0	85	132	20.0	14.0	0	57.0	0
1961	22	1 of 52	0	0	0	0	135	0	200		19.0	30.0	0	185.6	0
1962	23	8 of 53	0	0	1	0	727	0	2,725	50	22.1	27.5	2	1046.0	0
1963	24	18 of 55	0	3	7	0	4529	0	5,550	25	17.4	12.8	16	3302.9	0
1964	25	24 of 62	0	2	9	0	4990	10	10,378	19	12.6	14.3	12	4120.6	0
1965	26	46 of 55	1	13	21	0	7734	166	26,586	10	11.1	13.5	23	5396.4	2
1966	27	14 of 49	0	3	7	0	3831	252	28,130	18	11.0	12.6	8	3944.1	2
1967	28	17 of 49	2	7	9	4	4114	908	57,911	20	5.1	16.1	8	3928.7	5
1968	29	21 of 49	6	12	12	4	5661	1215	138,051	17	3.6	11.8	12	5746.6	6
1969	30	19 of 54	2	7	8	6	4341	946	75,065	23	3.8	16.8	8	5484.3	4

Career statistics (Continued)

1970	31	19 of 48	3	11	13	4	5034	906	117,600	34	4.8	10.7	11	6237.0	4
1971	32	4 of 48	0	0	1	0	564	13	3,844	51	17.8	24.2	1	961.4	0
1972	33	5 of 31	0	1	4	0	1196	9	11,667	2	11.8	13.0	4	1968.2	0
1973	34	28 of 28	4	16	19	5	9314	3167	267,513	2	4.5	10.0	20	9750.9	8
1974	35	30 of 30	10	21	22	3	9398	3530	363,781	2	3.9	6.7	23	11058.3	16
1975	36	27 of 30	3	13	13	3	7353	2542	214,691	9	6.5	14.8	13	8099.6	5
1976	37	30 of 30	9	22	23	2	9269	3791	453,404	1	5.1	8.2	25	10546.9	15
1977	38	30 of 30	9	25	27	3	9747	3219	561,641	1	4.0	4.5	30	11382.0	19
1978	39	30 of 30	10	23	24	8	9758	3587	623,506	1	3.6	6.0	28	11366.1	18
1979	40	31 of 31	4	19	22	1	9677	1323	440,128	4	5.3	8.6	25	11191.7	12
1980	41	31 of 31	6	19	22	14	9440	2810	567,890	2	3.1	9.0	26	11015.1	16
1981	42	18 of 31	2	6	10	2	4922	769	150,840	24	9.2	13.1	11	7133.5	6
1982	43	16 of 30	3	8	8	2	3439	379	231,590	27	8.8	15.8	8	5641.6	7
1983	44	16 of 30	4	4	8	3	3783	608	265,035	28	8.0	16.6	8	5974.6	4
1984	45	16 of 30	3	10	10	4	4387	736	403,853	22	7.4	7.4	14	7140.1	9
1985	46	16 of 28	2	6	7	0	3450	664	310,465	26	9.4	18.6	7	5675.2	6
1986	47	16 of 29	0	2	5	1	3467	110	137,010	29	12.8	21.3	6	5828.3	2
1987	48	16 of 29	0	2	4	0	2671	11	111,025	29	20.2	24.8	7	4519.4	3

Career statistics (Continued)

| 1988 | 49 | 10 of 29 | 0 | 0 | 3 | 0 | 144,948 | 31,677 | 66,065 | 38 | 26.9 | 23.5 | 6 | 3168.8 | 1 |
| 31 years | 560 | 83 | 255 | 319 | 69 | 1653 | 6 | 5,646,479 | | 8.2 | 12.6 | 362 | 172214.7 | 170 | |

IROC

1975

Race	Site	Cars	St	Fin	#	Sponsor / Owner	Car	Laps	Money	Status	Led
1	Michigan	12	8	2		NASCAR	Chevrolet	50/50	0	running	
2	Riverside	12	11	8		NASCAR	Chevrolet	30/30	0	running	
3	Riverside	12	5	9		NASCAR	Chevrolet	30/30	0	running	
4	Daytona	9	7	3		NASCAR	Chevrolet	40/40	0	running	

4 starts, 150 of 150 laps completed (100.0%), 0 laps led

Win:	0 (0.0%)	Average start: 7.8	Total Winnings: $0
Top 5:	2 (50.0%)	Average finish: 5.5	(excluding bonuses)
Top 10:	4 (100.0%)	DNF: 0	

IROC (Continued)

1977 (Continued)

	Race	Site	Cars	St	Fin	#	Sponsor / Owner	Car	Laps	Money	Status	Led
1	Michigan		12	11	9		NASCAR	Chevrolet	49/50	0	running	
2	Riverside		12	10	9		NASCAR	Chevrolet	29/30	0	running	0
3	Riverside		12	9	1		NASCAR	Chevrolet	30/30	0	running	30
4	Daytona		9	5	1		NASCAR	Chevrolet	40/40	0	running	

4 starts, 148 of 150 laps completed (98.7%), 30 laps led

Win: 2 (50.0%)	Average start: 8.8	Total Winnings: $0
Top 5: 2 (50.0%)	Average finish: 5.0	(excluding bonuses)
Top 10: 4 (100.0%)	DNF: 0	

1978

	Race	Site	Cars	St	Fin	#	Sponsor / Owner	Car	Laps	Money	Status	Led
1	Michigan		12	2	2		NASCAR	Chevrolet	50/50	0	running	
2	Riverside		12	12	10		NASCAR	Chevrolet	30/30	0	running	0
3	Riverside		12	3	1		NASCAR	Chevrolet	30/30	0	running	
4	Daytona		9	7	4		NASCAR	Chevrolet	40/40	0	running	

4 starts, 150 of 150 laps completed (100.0%), 0 laps led

Win: 1 (25.0%)   Average start: 6.0   Total Winnings: $0

IROC (Continued)

1978 (Continued)

Race Site	Cars	St	Fin	#	Sponsor / Owner	Car	Laps	Money	Status	Led
Top 5: 3 (75.0%)	Average finish: 4.2				(excluding bonuses)					
Top 10: 4 (100.0%)	DNF: 0									

1979

Race Site	Cars	St	Fin	#	Sponsor / Owner	Car	Laps	Money	Status	Led
1 Michigan	8	7	2		NASCAR	Chevrolet	50/50	0	running	
4 Riverside	12	5	2		NASCAR	Chevrolet	30/30	0	running	0
5 Atlanta	11	2	4		NASCAR	Chevrolet	66/66	0	running	

3 starts, 146 of 146 laps completed (100.0%), 0 laps led

Win: 0 (0.0%)	Average start: 4.7	Total Winnings: $0		
Top 5: 3 (100.0%)	Average finish: 2.7	(excluding bonuses)		
Top 10: 3 (100.0%)	DNF: 0			

1980

Race Site	Cars	St	Fin	#	Sponsor / Owner	Car	Laps	Money	Status	Led
1 Michigan	8	3	5		NASCAR	Chevrolet	50/50	0	running	

1 start, 50 of 50 laps completed (100.0%), 0 laps led

IROC (Continued)

1980 (Continued)

Race Site	Cars	St	Fin	#	Sponsor / Owner	Car	Laps	Money	Status	Led

Win:	0 (0.0%)	Average start: 3.0	Total Winnings: $0
Top 5:	1 (100.0%)	Average finish: 5.0	(excluding bonuses)
Top 10:	1 (100.0%)	DNF: 0	

1984

Race Site	Cars	St	Fin	#	Sponsor / Owner	Car	Laps	Money	Status	Led
1 Michigan	12	8	12		NASCAR	Chevrolet	49/50	0	running	0
2 Cleveland	12	1	1		NASCAR	Chevrolet	30/30	0	running	6
3 Talladega	12	9	2		NASCAR	Chevrolet	38/38	0	running	0
4 Michigan	12	2	2		NASCAR	Chevrolet	50/50	0	running	49

4 starts, 167 of 168 laps completed (99.4%), 55 laps led

Win:	1 (25.0%)	Average start: 5.0	Total Winnings: $0
Top 5:	3 (75.0%)	Average finish: 4.2	(excluding bonuses)
Top 10:	3 (75.0%)	DNF: 0	

256

1985

Race	Site	Cars	St	Fin	#	Sponsor / Owner	Car	Laps	Money	Status	Led
1	Daytona	12	7	6		NASCAR	Chevrolet	40/40	0	running	4
2	Mid-Ohio	12	7	12		NASCAR	Chevrolet	29/29	0	running	0
3	Michigan	12	9	3		NASCAR	Chevrolet	50/50	0	running	0

3 starts, 119 of 119 laps completed (100.0%), 4 laps led

Win:	0 (0.0%)	Average start: 7.7	Total Winnings: $0
Top 5:	1 (33.3%)	Average finish: 7.0	(excluding bonuses)
Top 10:	2 (66.7%)	DNF: 0	

1986

Race	Site	Cars	St	Fin	#	Sponsor / Owner	Car	Laps	Money	Status	Led
1	Daytona	12	8	2		NASCAR	Chevrolet	40/40	0	running	0
2	Mid-Ohio	12	11	10		NASCAR	Chevrolet	29/29	0	running	0
3	Talladega	12	7	1		NASCAR	Chevrolet	38/38	0	running	30
4	Watkins Glen	12	1	6		NASCAR	Chevrolet	30/30	0	running	0

4 starts, 137 of 137 laps completed (100.0%), 30 laps led

Win:	1 (25.0%)	Average start: 6.8	Total Winnings: $0
Top 5:	2 (50.0%)	Average finish: 4.8	(excluding bonuses)
Top 10:	4 (100.0%)	DNF: 0	

INDY 500

Year	Car	Start	Qual	Rank	Finish	Laps	Led	Retired
1966	66	24	159.794	15	28	0	0	Crash FS
1967	21	20	162.830	30	17	176	0	Crash T3
1971	21	14	170.770	19	16	140	0	Cam Cover
1972	21	32	178.864	33	10	193	0	Flagged
Totals						509	0	

Starts	4
Poles	0
Front Row	0
Wins	0
Top 5	0
Top 10	1
Retired	3

OWNERSHIP RECORD

Year	Driver	Races	Win	T5	T10	Pole	Laps	Led	Earnings	Rank	AvSt	AvFn	RAF	Miles	LLF
1987	Cale Yarborough	16	0	2	4	0	2671	11	111,025	29	20.2	24.8	7	4519.4	3
1988	Dale Jarrett	19	0	0	1	0	5361	4	118,640	23	22.3	21.8	11	5511.6	2
1988	Cale Yarborough	10	0	0	3	0	1653	6	66,065	38	26.9	23.5	6	3168.8	1
1989	Dale Jarrett	29	0	2	5	0	7798	99	232,317	24	24.2	22.7	18	9177.6	3
1990	Dick Trickle	29	0	2	4	1	8311	82	350,990	22	14.5	21.9	16	9926.7	3
1991	Chuck Bown	1	0	0	0	0	391	0	5,225	76	31.0	26.0	1	244.4	0
1991	Randy LaJoie	3	0	0	0	0	926	0	23,875	50	28.7	29.0	1	1061.5	0
1991	Dorsey Schroeder	1	0	0	0	0	2	0	11,945	59	36.0	41.0	0	3.0	0
1991	Lake Speed	20	0	0	0	0	4513	0	149,300	32	19.9	25.3	10	5051.8	2

OWNERSHIP RECORD (Continued)

Year	Driver													
1991	Dick Trickle	4	0	0	0	0	1362	0	129,125	35	21.8	20.8	4	1735.6	0
1992	Jimmy Hensley	22	0	0	4	0	6804	22	247,660	28	17.4	18.2	21	8491.0	2
1992	Bobby Hillin, Jr.	1	0	0	0	0	393	0	102,160	34	32.0	25.0	1	245.6	0
1992	Chad Little	6	0	0	0	0	1852	0	145,805	31	24.2	27.2	4	1908.6	0
1993	Derrike Cope	30	0	1	0	0	8406	38	402,515	26	18.1	23.6	22	9965.2	2
1994	Derrike Cope	16	0	0	0	0	4261	7	398,436	30	22.9	28.8	9	5028.7	0
1994	Jeremy Mayfield	12	0	0	0	0	3452	0	226,265	37	32.0	25.2	9	4303.8	0
1995	Jeremy Mayfield	27	0	1	0	1	7943	79	436,805	31	23.7	22.0	25	10441.6	3
1996	John Andretti	8	0	1	1	1	3018	1	688,511	31	19.0	23.4	7	2813.4	1
1996	Jeremy Mayfield	23	0	2	2	1	5862	20	592,853	26	22.7	22.1	19	7844.9	7
1997	John Andretti	32	1	3	1	0	9334	135	1,143,725	23	23.0	23.6	29	11972.5	6
1998	Rich Bickle	21	0	1	1	0	5691	0	682,255	39	25.5	26.3	16	6939.1	3
1998	Greg Sacks	7	0	0	0	0	1821	0	296,880	53	23.6	35.3	5	2312.4	0
1999	Rick Mast	34	0	2	0	0	9487	25	1,290,143	32	21.9	26.6	34	12540.2	6
13 years		371	1	13	32	3	101,312	529	7,852,520		21.9	24.0	275	125207.3	44

NOTES

Many of the stories relayed herein were from Cale's own recollections, as relayed to Bill Neely in his autobiography *Cale: The Hazardous Life and Times of America's Greatest Stock Car Driver.*

Additional information compiled from, but not limited to, the following websites:

www.racing-reference.info/driver

"The Top 10 Daytona 500s Ever ...": Woody, Larry; http://entertainment.howstuffworks.com/top-10-daytona-500s9.htm

www.nascar.com

www.grantwcooper.com/Cale_Yarborough.html

www.motorsportshalloffame.com

www.tv.com

www.racestrl.com